# RAISE YOUR
# VIBRATION

# RAISE YOUR VIBRATION

### 111 PRACTICES TO INCREASE YOUR SPIRITUAL CONNECTION

## KYLE GRAY

**HAY HOUSE**

Carlsbad, California • New York City • London • Sydney
Johannesburg • Vancouver • Hong Kong • New Delhi

**First published and distributed in the United Kingdom by:**
Hay House UK Ltd, Astley House, 33 Notting Hill Gate, London W11 3JQ
Tel: +44 (0)20 3675 2450; Fax: +44 (0)20 3675 2451;
www.hayhouse.co.uk

**Published and distributed in the United States of America by:**
Hay House Inc., PO Box 5100, Carlsbad, CA 92018-5100
Tel: (1) 760 431 7695 or (800) 654 5126
Fax: (1) 760 431 6948 or (800) 650 5115; www.hayhouse.com

**Published and distributed in Australia by:**
Hay House Australia Ltd, 18/36 Ralph St, Alexandria NSW 2015
Tel: (61) 2 9669 4299; Fax: (61) 2 9669 4144; www.hayhouse.com.au

**Published and distributed in the Republic of South Africa by:**
Hay House SA (Pty) Ltd, PO Box 990, Witkoppen 2068
info@hayhouse.co.za; www.hayhouse.co.za

**Published and distributed in India by:**
Hay House Publishers India, Muskaan Complex, Plot No.3, B-2,
Vasant Kunj, New Delhi 110 070
Tel: (91) 11 4176 1620; Fax: (91) 11 4176 1630; www.hayhouse.co.in

**Distributed in Canada by:**
Raincoast Books, 2440 Viking Way, Richmond, B.C. V6V 1N2
Tel: (1) 604 448 7100; Fax: (1) 604 270 7161; www.raincoast.com

A catalogue record for this book is available from the British Library.

ISBN: 978-1-78180-510-7

Interior images: 40, 60, 84, 106, 126, 148, 165, 172, 192, 216, 234, 244
Thinkstock/AnVino; 49, 80, 102 Liron Gilenberg | www.ironicitalics.com

Printed and bound by CPI Group (UK) Ltd, Croydon, CR0 4YY

# CONTENTS

*Soul note*     vii

*Acknowledgements*     ix

*Introduction*     xi

Feel the vibes     1

Raise your vibes     5

The universe is recruiting you!     13

Vibes in the body     23

How to use this book     31

    **Ground:** Vibes 1–10     39

    **Flow:** Vibes 11–20     59

    **Ignite:** Vibes 21–30     83

    **Receive:** Vibes 31–40     105

    **Express:** Vibes 41–50     125

    **See:** Vibes 51–60     147

    **Know:** Vibes 61–70     171

    **Light Up!** Vibes 71–80     191

    **Manifest:** Vibes 81–90     215

    **Integrate:** Vibes 91–100     233

    **Activate:** Vibes 101–111     243

Your lightworker declaration     255

*About the author*     259

# SOUL NOTE

I started my spiritual journey young. I was 15 when I officially delved into the universe looking for answers and the meaning of life. Every day I would dedicate time to reading, writing and meditating – it just seemed the most magical thing to do. Today I am frequently asked how I'm 'so psychic' or how I maintain my upbeat nature, and the answer is the same every time: daily spiritual practice.

Having a daily spiritual practice is the key to developing your spiritual skills, gifts and qualities. When you take the time to acknowledge who you are, focus your mind and meditate, you create room in your life to grow and you encourage your heart to open up and connect deeply with the flow of life.

I like to imagine the mind as a garden. If you leave a garden untended, it will begin to grow wild in certain areas. There will be weeds, and many of the beautiful flowers will wilt and fade away. But if you take the time to look after the garden by fertilizing the soil, planting new seeds and encouraging growth in the areas that have been bare, you will begin to see the rewards of your commitment.

It's just the same with your mind – when you plant the right seeds, they will begin to grow. Your mind is the space where you can cultivate a spiritual practice and connect to your body and soul.

So often people who have read my books, come to my demonstrations or participated in my workshops have asked me which books, tools, card decks and crystals are the best for maintaining a spiritual connection. It's almost as though people believe there are tricks or short cuts that will help them get there faster, but really that's not true – in fact it's an *illusion*.

One of my favourite yoga masters, Sri K. Pattabhi Jois, once said, 'Yoga is 99 per cent practice and 1 per cent theory', and he was absolutely right. The same goes for spirituality: if you want to create a deep and meaningful spiritual connection, you *must* do the practice. So this book is a response to all of the questions I've been asked and an encouraging kick in the butt to help you develop your daily spiritual practice.

Over the 12 years since I started my journey I've explored many schools of thought, energy therapies and types of meditation. Now I've brought together all I've learned to create a daily spiritual practice for you, so all you have to do is follow in the footsteps I have created.

The truth is, as sages past and present have said, that *you* have the answers you seek. *You* have the magic, the miracles, the power and the tools – they're all there right in the centre of your heart. That's where you'll find what you're looking for. My prayer is that this book will act as a map guiding you back to the core of your being so that you can experience the love that sits gently within your heart.

May you tend the garden of your mind and may the sunshine of your soul help your seeds to grow and create a life that is filled with joy and love.

**KYLE GRAY**
Mysore, India
January 2015

# ACKNOWLEDGEMENTS

I'm super grateful to be in this position – sharing my fifth book with the world – and it feels so good. I'd like to thank everyone at Hay House for giving me this wonderful opportunity to share my vision with the world and ultimately live my dream.

Special thanks to Michelle Pilley, my incredible commissioning editor and the MD of Hay House UK, for creating a space (and supporting its growth) for people like me to do what we do. Michelle, you are a huge blessing.

Also shouts and bundles of good vibes to Lizzie Henry (my editor/ general words magician/Earth angel), Leanne Anastasi for the incredible cover and internal design (those lil' vibes around the title of each lesson as sooooo cool) and Julie Oughton for helping all suggestions meet in the same place and bringing the whole thing together.

Love and thanks to Jo Burgess, Ruth Tewkesbury (love u) and Tom Cole for the publicity and social media support – I love that you all give me a kick in the butt when I need it. Also thanks to Jessica Gibson for helping me create and cultivate my speaking platform – you da bomb.

I also want to use this space to thank Greta Lipp and the whole Wrage family for really helping me share my vision and ideas in the German-speaking countries – I have a whole new Euro family whom I absolutely adore.

Thank you angels for gracing me with your presence daily, for reminding me of the light and for helping me shine as bright as I do. You are my spiritual homies and I will never not be obsessed by how much love you share in this world. Thank you, thank you, thank you.

To the universe – I humbly bow. You are my essence; you are the light within the light and the everything that is. Thanks for blowing my mind like every-effing-day. It's so cool.

Finally thanks to my Mum for rocking the business with me – for doing everything you do and helping me be who I am today. I love, love, love, love you!

# INTRODUCTION

There's one thing that psychics and scientists can agree on: everything in the universe is made up of energy. That includes you. Right now there is energy moving through every cell of your body, every atom of the air that you're breathing and every part of the chair that you're sitting on. Energy is alive. It's here and it's now. It's what we're made of and it connects us to everything that was, is and ever will be.

Energy is a subtle vibration, but it moves quickly. It's completely neutral, but it responds to our emotions and actions, and we respond in turn. We all know what it's like to walk into a room and be met by a 'bad vibe'. If a drama's kicked off at a party just before we've turned up, we'll feel something in our belly swirling round and telling us to move away or even leave. It's the opposite when we experience a 'good vibe', for instance when we meet a friend we haven't seen in forever – we feel so happy in their presence we don't want to leave. The truth is, we all respond to the vibrations around us.

The almighty universe we live in responds as well when we put our own vibes out there. It's as if the world around us is one huge mirror and it's reflecting every thought we've had, every emotion we've felt and every action we've taken. Our outer world is a huge reflection of our inner beliefs and the beliefs of those surrounding us in our life.

You are here reading this now because you've made a conscious decision to live a more meaningful life. The universe has heard your call and it's ready to support you every step of the way.

In order to live a more meaningful life, a life of purpose, joy and fulfilment, first you have to believe it's possible. The almighty universe does want us all to be fulfilled in every possible way, but it honours our free will. We were sent to this Earth to experience a good life, but it's something we have to choose. So we need to raise our vibrations. Then our external world will begin to reflect the loving feelings we are cultivating within and we'll begin to experience a life beyond our wildest dreams.

The time has come. If you're ready to fly high, all you have to do is get spiritually high! Let me show you how to raise your vibration...

# FEEL THE VIBES

'*Energy cannot be created or destroyed, it can only be changed from one form to another.*'

ALBERT EINSTEIN

Ever since I was a child I've been able to feel things about people, animals and places – it just seems to be there. It's there for all of us in fact – from early childhood, you too have had the ability to recognize changes in the atmosphere surrounding you. Your intuitive perception has been able to pick up danger, sadness, love and laughter. I've had this tenfold. For me, there's a feeling, then all of a sudden there's a deep knowing that something is right or wrong. For years I was desperate to turn these natural senses off because they felt *un*natural.

In truth, being able to feel what's going on around us is so natural that it's something most of us take for granted. That doesn't mean we act on it. We all know what it's like to blurt out the words 'I knew that was going to happen' or 'I should have just listened to myself' because earlier we'd felt something change or something inviting *us* to change. I believe that 'something' is a vibration. It's energy.

Ever since high school I've been fascinated by Eastern belief systems, especially Hinduism and Buddhism. These amazing religions talk about a vibrational sound that created the universe, an energy they call 'Om' or 'Aum'. Scientists, on the other hand, can't put their finger on exactly what created the universe, or what it's made of, and may even call it 'nothingness'. Whatever you like to call it, it's real, it's there and we all know it. We can feel it because we're part of it.

## Highs and lows

We interpret energy through our feelings. Have you ever turned up accidentally at an event where everyone was dancing and laughing? Have you ever seen people laughing and just had to join in? The laughter fills every part of your being – you feel your heart expand and you forget all your worries and cares. You feel alive. This is a high vibration.

When you know you're in danger, though, you feel your shoulders begin to round and your head comes down to protect your precious heart. You want to curl up into a ball. This is a low vibration.

In order to recognize a high vibration, we have to have experienced the low. That doesn't mean we have to stay with the low, of course. How can we get high?

## How high are you?

Although things happen in life and nature takes its course, we have a choice about how we feel and what sort of energy we give off. Every thought we think and every choice we make determines our vibration.

I love His Holiness the Dalai Lama – I just think he's rad. He's such a dude. I remember going to see him in Edinburgh with my friend Diane. I was overwhelmed by his presence. This man travels constantly around the world and shares his teachings with hundreds, thousands and millions each year, yet he seems to maintain his powerful smile and an energy that I can only describe as golden.

I remember thinking how amazing it would be to shine so brightly. I thought about it for a while before it dawned on me that the Dalai Lama was someone who had dedicated his whole life to a daily spiritual practice and the only way to shine as brightly as he did was to follow my own.

## What is a daily spiritual practice?

So, let's get this straight, because I don't want you feeling guilty or frustrated before we even get started. I know for a fact that many people get themselves wound up and annoyed because they find it difficult to maintain a meditation practice or make it to the yoga class they signed up for on time. And let me tell you, I have been in those shoes!

A daily spiritual practice (DSP) is a choice you make. It's also a massive opportunity to recognize that you are more than just a body. It can be a chosen time daily when you sit in meditation as part of a yoga practice or an energy-healing session you give yourself. Although to be honest a DSP isn't something you do once a day, it's more an intention you have for the day.

You also invite yourself to recognize that intention at intervals throughout the day. This is because it's so easy to start the day with positive intentions but then come across challenges or setbacks in the 'real world' that just make you forget what you intended. But when you cultivate that garden of your mind – when you begin your day by sowing the seeds of your intention and every time you come back to them during the day you invite them to grow – you will soon have beautiful flowers blooming in your mind and their sweet fragrance will spread through your life.

So, to keep it real and simple – because that's really what spirituality is all about – a daily spiritual practice is setting positive intentions in your mind and coming back to them throughout the day to remind yourself of them and receive any internal guidance that is being offered to you.

Through maintaining a daily spiritual practice you will begin to raise your vibrations so that you give off bright, light and happy energy and experience the peace you deserve to feel and the life you deserve to live.

## Spirituality and religion

Your daily spiritual practice doesn't have to involve a god or a religion, by the way. It's more about you and your connection to the universe. If you have a religious practice then you can combine it with what we're doing here – there will be no conflict with your belief system because I'm simply encouraging you to recognize your light and feel more in touch with your own divinity.

Personally, I say I have no religion. Saying I follow one religion seems limiting when I'm fascinated by the fact there are *so many* roads of love and the divine out there. I am not religious, I am spiritual!

I do feel comfortable with the word 'God', but to make that energy feel more universal and open, I will call it 'the universe' or 'the divine' here, because it's not one thing – it's everything.

Let's start now by looking in more detail at raising your vibration and what it can do for you.

# RAISE YOUR VIBES

*'If you will change your mind concerning anything and absolutely keep it changed, that thing must and will change too.'*

Emmet Fox

You are the creator of your world. Everything you think, feel and express is literally moving out into the universe and creating the path before you. A thought is like a ripple when you drop a pebble into the water – it moves out and away from you, creating movements and changes in the field surrounding you.

Your thoughts are creating waves in your life. Just as a ripple moves out on the tide and comes back in a wave, so your thoughts come back to you. For that reason, you want to choose thoughts that are working for you, not against you.

We know that our thoughts are expressions of our feelings and we know that when we think about something we love, we feel good on the inside. We also know what it's like to be plagued by something in our past. If we continue to think about it, we can be led into a state of deep despair.

Raising your vibes includes replacing the old thoughts you have about yourself and your life with better ones. And when you change your thoughts, you change your world.

I first heard about changing your thoughts through Louise Hay. She was one of the first spiritual authors I read and I instantly fell in love with her. In her life-changing work Louise helps us realize that we are literally writing our own story – we can choose to think loving thoughts about our life or we can choose to be stuck in fear. Essentially it's our choice, but we know that one is going to be better than the other.

I recently did a talk in Freiburg, Germany, and a lady asked me for some guidance regarding her life. She wanted to know if it was her karma to spend the rest of her life without a partner. She was sitting in the front row with her three children, who were all in their teens, and as I looked at her, my heart burst with love. I knew instantly what was going on for her – she had been let down regularly in her life and in her relationships. As I tuned in to her vibration, I realized there was an unconscious story running in her mind and in her life.

Marion had been divorced after a long struggle in her marriage. Her husband had been unfaithful and had spent more time in 'the office' than he had with Marion and their children. Ultimately, he had let down his family, who had desperately wanted his love and approval, and the rejection had begun to affect Marion on an emotional level. Even though on the outside she was a great source of strength for her family, on the inside she felt worthless and alone.

When I tapped into her energy I could feel that she was telling herself a story much darker than the truth: she was saying that she wasn't a good woman and she must have done something wrong. And at the same time she was feeling victimized and asking herself daily, 'Why did this happen to me?' and even 'What have I done to deserve this?'

I told her, with as much diplomacy as possible, about her current thoughts and situation – and added that I knew exactly how to change it.

I could feel Marion's angels holding her up and knew they were singing her praises. They wanted to thank her for being the loyal one and putting her family before herself. I told her this and how amazing she was as a person.

Then I discovered the thought process that was ultimately standing between Marion and a loving and supportive relationship.

'You became so used to being rejected and hurt in your marriage that now you expect it from all relationships,' I told her. 'That's why you aren't manifesting a relationship in your life – because you're expecting to be hurt and you know for certain you don't want to be hurt again. This is placing huge walls around your heart and they are blocking you off from the love you deserve. You see, my friend, you deserve to love and be loved. You don't have to do anything in order for it to occur and you don't have to "work hard" to get it. Experiencing love is your divine right!'

At that moment Marion broke down and let go of much of the pain she was holding inside. Clairvoyantly I could see shadow energy (which had been created in her own mind) leaving her and golden light coming in and surrounding her. This was symbolic of her vibration rising.

Marion told me, 'You're right – I'm desperate for a relationship, but I have the feeling that I'm just going to be hurt again and it makes sense that that is acting as a block. But I'm ready to change the way I think and I'm grateful you have shown me how.'

Realizing what is preventing us from having the life we want is always the first step, but it's not the miracle. The miracle lies in our capacity to change the way we think and rewrite our inner story. In this case, Marion had to recognize that she was deserving of love but also that not everyone was out to hurt her. She was encouraged to realize that she was a force of love and could raise her vibration and manifest the life she deserved.

## The universe

The universe is a beautiful thing. It's basically energy that is responding to our free will and most of the time we don't even realize it. We don't understand that we get to choose what sort of energy we give off, receive and surround ourselves with. It's not a case of going, 'I like that energy – give me that, please,' it's more how we feel that makes the choice for us. For example, if you're going around feeling like a failure, then failing is going to be your story. If you're going around feeling happy and contented even with small things, then you'll continue along that pathway.

The universe is unlimited and has so much to offer us, but we live in a world of limitations. It sounds crazy when you think about it, but we're led to believe that we can't have what we want and even that we can lose everything we do have. That's nothing but an *illusion*.

By choosing to raise our vibration, we are making a decision to move into a place that is filled with unlimited potential. We're choosing to accept the unlimited energy the universe is willing to offer us.

Energy is never-ending – it will never cease to be. Even when our body dies, our energy will continue to live on. We are all part of the oneness of life and can move from the physical to the non-physical. Does that feel like a loss? It's not a loss – when we move to a non-physical state, we are moving back to our natural state of being.

The point is that when we accept that we are limitless and that we are always one with everything, we allow limitless possibility into our life. And that includes miracles.

# Miracles

According to the metaphysical text *A Course in Miracles*, 'Miracles occur naturally as expressions of love.' But so many of us find it hard to believe in them, and certainly don't feel that we deserve them. Why?

We've been brought up in a world that measures everything and judges accordingly. So, other people measure up what we own, how much money we earn, what clothes we wear, what we look like, and so on, and we do the same. Generally this measuring system makes us feel that we're not complete or not good enough. These feelings begin to write our inner story and the inner story tells us that we don't deserve miracles. Anyway, miracles are limited – if we receive one, we're depriving someone else of one. And that's not fair.

It's time to change this. It's time to rewrite this story and cultivate a life that fulfils us on all levels – a life that is constantly open to miracles.

What's more, we can all have miracles. *A Course in Miracles* also says:

> *'Miracles are not in competition, and the number of them that you can do is limitless.'*

You deserve miracles in your life simply because you exist. As far as I'm concerned, we are all miracles in the first place and we can all create them in our life.

Quite simply, a miracle is a shift in perception – it's a change in the way we think and ultimately it's a change in our life. It doesn't have to be a dramatic outer event – it can be a subtle inner shift that creates a feeling of wholeness and richness in our life.

No miracle is greater or smaller than the next. The changing of our thoughts is no greater miracle than the appearance of a holy master. Letting go of the measuring system is important here. If we see something as greater, we make it inaccessible in our mind, and if our mind creates our world, that means we make it inaccessible in our life.

Here's a thought that has helped me. It's from my journal:

> *'It's not how big the miracle is – it's how much room you make for it.'*

When you raise your vibration, you make room for miracles in your life. You prepare the space within yourself to receive love and support from the universe. And when you create a daily spiritual practice, you are basically taking the time to remind yourself that you deserve to be supported and you deserve miracles.

## Spirit soaring

When you walk into a room to be met by a loved one you haven't seen in a while, you feel overwhelmed with excitement. Your heart bursts open and you feel a deep sense of connectedness. On a bodily level, you want to hug them. You want to grab their hand, look into their eyes and smile. On a soul (vibrational) level, there's a sense of recognition going on. Your soul knows theirs, you feel their light and you experience it within you.

The feeling of love that overwhelms you at such moments is something extremely special – it's a reminder of your natural state. Your natural state is one of high vibration – that's why it feels so good to love and be loved. Love is the very highest of vibrations and it's what the universe is operating on. Anything that isn't love – like fear or encountering an energy that is 'negative' – makes us feel on edge or want to walk in the opposite direction. That's because this is the energy that is the furthest away from our natural state.

When you begin to raise your vibration, you follow what feels most natural to you. You spend less time on what feels uncomfortable, and if you do feel uncomfortable, a shift of thoughts and feelings occurs that guides you back to your natural state.

To give you an example, I love snowboarding and I love yoga. Both bring me a deep sense of excitement. Whether I'm practising yoga on a mat or I'm coming down a mountain at top speed, I feel a rush of life within me. I feel that I have everything and can do anything – essentially, I feel limitless. In this state of sheer delight I become connected to possibility, I raise my vibration and I attune to the universe. I can also direct my energy into what's working for me and let go of what's not. I'm able to set intentions and work towards my goals.

## Gratitude

So, high vibes are a natural state that we experience when we're doing something we love or are surrounded by people we love. We also can move into this state by being grateful.

Gratitude is a miracle in itself. It's a phenomenal recognition of what we have and it makes us feel full. And seeing that our cup isn't full but overflowing will raise our vibrations even more.

When I work with audiences, I set the intention that whatever we gain from the experience will be to the benefit of all sentient beings through time and space. Through service we are raising our vibration because we are offering whatever kindness we feel or whatever blessings we receive to others.

I also encourage each member of the audience to think about someone or something in their life that they are grateful for. Through gratitude we are moving back to the heart and experiencing love. And love has the highest vibration of all...

# THE UNIVERSE IS RECRUITING YOU!

> '*Spiritual advancement is not measured by one's outward powers, but only by the depth of his bliss in meditation.*'
>
> PARAMAHANSA YOGANANDA

Have you seen the signs? Have you seen repetitive numbers on your clock, phone, car dashboard, even a receipt from the store? Numbers like 1:11, 2:22, 3:33? Personally, I've seen them everywhere. It even started to freak out my friends at one point when my full tank of fuel kept coming to perfect number sequences like £44.44. At first I thought that these sequences were angels saying hello, but in more recent times I've come to realize that there's a larger-scale operation going on. These numbers aren't coincidences – they are messages from the universe inviting us to be ambassadors of positive change, or what people know as *lightworkers*.

A lightworker is someone who is here to make a positive difference to the world. I believe that before coming to Earth, all lightworkers consciously chose to awaken at this time to direct the world into a new age that would be honest and filled with peace, and know a love that was divine.

There is also a call of need moving through the universe at this time. Your own need to create a life of integrity and love is also something you chose before you came here. And your conscious choice to make your life more positive is actually your response to the inner call of the universe.

# 11:11/111

I'm not going to lie – when I started seeing the numbers 111 or 11:11 recurring in my life, I *knew* there was some sort of spiritual meaning behind it, but it took me a while to figure out what it was, because when I googled it (which is what I do with everything I don't understand), there were so many interpretations of it.

I remember getting an 11:11 on my iPhone screen one day and deciding to meditate on what its message was for me. What I received was clear, precise and, to be honest, simple.

The message that I came to know deep within me was nothing new. It was an age-old message that we have heard from great spiritual teachers like Jesus and ancient sages like Patanjali (who compiled the *Yoga Sutras*). It was this:

### *We are all one.*

As I said, it's nothing new. But when you receive your 11:11 message, you are literally in touch with the divine. You are connecting to everyone/thing that ever was, is and will be. And as you are connecting to that frequency, it's important to focus your thoughts on something that is contributing to the growth, healing and nurturing of the world.

We all have challenging thoughts and we all feel disconnected and frustrated from time to time – and this doesn't make us a bad person or a terrible lightworker, because we are here to grow and learn. But when the 11:11 arrives, it's a call from the source of creation, the depths of our soul, the angels and the universe itself to lift up our energy, raise our vibration and step into the light to become a guide, leader and teacher to the world.

## *The I AM-ness*

When it comes to being a lightworker, there is a real call from the universe for us to honour who we truly are. We are a soul within a body and we are here to make a difference. When we accept the spiritual gift and mission we have been given, we awaken and empower ourselves from the inside out. Accepting and embracing who we truly are is what I like to call 'the I AM-ness', but it is also called 'the I AM presence' by various other schools of thought.

This isn't new information either – it has been taught for thousands of years. In the Bible Jesus used the words 'I am the light of the world', which is basically what a lightworker is.

When you awaken and align your I AM-ness, you are basically acknowledging that you are part of something greater than you are. This is exactly what happens when you see 111 or 11:11 on the clock – you are invited by heaven to acknowledge and accept that you are part of all that is.

Before delving any further into this book, why not take a few moments to awaken and align your I AM-ness by doing this exercise.

✦ Take a deep breath in and then slowly exhale. Say:

### *'I am the light.'*

✦ Imagine yourself covered in brilliant white light.

✦ Take another deep breath in and then slowly exhale. Say:

### *'You are the light.'*

✦ Imagine everyone everywhere lighting up.

✦ Take another deep breath in and then slowly exhale. Say:

### *'We are the light.'*

✦ See your light and everyone else's light coming together.

I love doing this. It's such a powerful and easy technique. If you ever need to do it really quickly to shift your vibes and move into who you are, you can simply say, 'I am, you are, we are!'

## Other signs

You may not have received a 11:11 sign but you may have received various other messages from the universe. That's totally cool. Or maybe you haven't received anything you could call a 'sign' but have a deep inner feeling that you need to be a 'better person'. If so, you're in the right place too.

### *12:34/1234*

Another common sequence that shows up is numbers moving in order. You might pick up the phone at 12:34, for instance, or see those numbers appearing somewhere else.

I like to call this 'the ladder'. It represents moving up the spiritual ladder: you are being told that you are taking the right steps to lift your heart and energy and make a positive change to the world.

## *22:22/222*

This one has a personal resonance with me because I see it so often and so does my best friend, Teri. Every time we see it on our phone we text each other, and that's most days.

When two number 2s face each other, they create a love-heart shape. I call the 2s facing each other 'swans of love', as they look like swans swimming across a lake. When you see this, it is the universe encouraging you to acknowledge the deep love that is within you.

While 11:11 is all about oneness, 22:22 is all about bringing that oneness together. It's that divine call from the universe inviting you to recognize that your intentions and actions influence others. Every single word you say, every deed you perform and every interaction you have with others is creating waves of change. When you see 22:22, you are being invited to see how you are the light in the room. How are your actions, deeds, intentions and words positively affecting all those around you? Turn on that light and shine bright.

## *3:33/333*

Thirty-three is an auspicious number in spirituality because it is believed that Jesus lived to this age. Not only that, in numerology it is known as the 'Master Teacher' number. For this reason it has become strongly associated with the ascended masters. Ascended masters are spiritual teachers and change agents who once walked the Earth but now offer their support, based on their life lessons, from the heart of the universe (heaven).

When 3:33/333 shows up it's telling you not only that you're a great leader of some kind but also that the leaders and teachers who have gone before you are encouraging you.

## 4:44/444

In traditional numerology, 44 was the number of structure. It became the number of business, planning and building strong foundations. In recent years it has become associated with angels, and boy, have those angels used it to their advantage. Thanks to Doreen Virtue, 44 has become the traditional number of cards in angel card decks and through her work 444 has become a widely recognized sign that angels are present. When I first learned this, I never stopped seeing 14:44 on my clock and I have woken up to interesting information at 4:44 a.m. several times over the years.

When you see this number, your angels want you to know that they are your biggest fans. The angelic realm is drawing close to you, offering you support and reminding you that you don't have to do everything on your own. Be open to the angels' light and help to feel more secure and in flow with your life.

## High-pitched noises

These are some of my favourite signs. I call a high-pitched noise a 'download' because I believe it shows we are receiving some sort of divine guidance from the universe. I like to imagine the human mind and body are like a huge radio that we can tune to receive different messages from heaven, ascended masters and angels. Sometimes our frequency isn't fully tuned in but still can pick up other channels, and when we hear a high-pitched noise we are being given a taster of what can be received.

I was recently in Colorado giving a talk and I spoke about the experience of hearing a high-pitched noise. To my surprise, at least 50 people came up to me afterwards to tell me that they'd heard these noises for years and had never understood what was happening.

When it happens to me (as it did earlier today, before I wrote this section), I take a moment or two just to acknowledge it. I come to the awareness that I am receiving some sort of guidance, download, upgrade or information from the angels and universe. Then I usually close my eyes and breathe for a moment and say this simple prayer from my book *Angel Prayers*: 'Thank you, angels, for revealing to me what I need to know!' Even if I don't hear or know anything else, I just trust that whatever I need to know will be revealed to me in due course.

The next time you hear a high-pitched noise, know that you are being invited to raise your vibes.

## *Hearing your name*

Hearing their name being called is a sign that freaks out a lot of people. Many people get the idea that there's some weird spirit following them – not true! When you hear your name being called, the universe is echoing the love it has for you. So, instead of having a huge debate in your mind about whether you are imagining it or not, just respond with 'I hear your call, universe!'

It's important to acknowledge that your name has a lot to do with your vibration. I recently had an interesting conversation with angel expert Diana Cooper when we were out for dinner with our publisher before the Angel World Summit. We were just engaging in general chit-chat about life and my favourite subject (food), and as I was chattering away, I shortened her name to 'Di'. I said, 'Sorry, Diana, I do that all the time, as my mum and one of my close friends are both called "Diane".'

Her reply was sweet but quite powerful at the same time. She said, 'That's okay. I was "Di" until I had my first angel experience and then I became "Diana".'

The truth was, I already knew that was right. In fact, trusting who you are and saying your name with love in your heart can be said to sum up everything that I've learned to this point on my spiritual path. There are many ways to do this, from the affirmation techniques that Louise Hay has shared with us to the self-acceptance we are encouraged to move into by our guardian angels. And angels love to say our name to us – that's why you'll hear your name being called out from time to time if you're needing a nudge to step into your light and move into your true power.

When you say your own name in a loving way, when you write your name in a loving way and when you ask others to respect your name, you initiate your 'I AM-ness'.

## What happens next?

So you've received the signs, you've heard the calls and you know that there's something larger going on. The universe has recruited you. It's pointed you out as a change agent and an Earth angel. You've been invited to lift your energy and that of all the people around you. The fact that you're here tells us that you've responded to that call and that you're ready to initiate the process.

Your life will now become a demonstration of how to live in the best way. It probably already is. You may already have heard that people love to be in your company, feel they can rely on you and know they can trust you with their deepest emotions. You've probably had strangers or people you hardly know tell you their entire life story, including things they've never been able to admit to others.

Your life is a demonstration because the positivity you activate within yourself becomes a platform for other people to get positive too. Your excitement and love for life are infectious, but not only that – the light that is shining within you will now get brighter and brighter, and all of those who surround you and who are drawn to you will begin to light up too.

In order to progress along this path, it's important to be clear with the universe, the angels and your guides that you accept this mission to light up. Don't worry, though – this doesn't mean that you have to quit your job or work 24/7 for the universe/angels/spirit world. It just means that you've accepted the call and you're willing to contribute towards the healing, peace and nurturing of the world. You're willing to raise your vibration.

# VIBES IN THE BODY

*'What lies behind us and what lies before us are
tiny matters compared to what lies within us.'*

ATTRIBUTED TO RALPH WALDO EMERSON

The physical body is the home of the soul and the space where the mind dwells. For that reason, the physical you needs loving care and attention so that it can support the raising of your vibration.

For many years I left my physical body behind. My spiritual practice was all centred on the soul and the mind. Everything I did on a spiritual level was loving and nourishing, but at the same time I *knew* deep within my bones that my body wasn't responding or representing the intentions I was making and the work I was doing on the inside.

I know that, like me, you've probably tried a million different health fads, eaten kale and even dabbled with being vegan. And I'm not here to lecture you on your diet, more to help you find a way of keeping the whole you (body, mind and soul) radiating at a higher vibration. I'll start by telling you what happened to me.

## 'The psychic diet'

From my teenage years I worked professionally doing spiritual readings and would be out doing them late into the evenings. All the lifting of my energy to read people's vibes and contact the spirit world would make me feel high and excited. I would go home via fast-food joints to pick up heavy, greasy and sludgy food that would bring me back to Earth. In the end I became reliant on heavy foods to switch off, go to sleep and slow down my overactive mind.

In truth, I thought this was how it worked. Most of the psychics I worked alongside and looked up to had their vices. They would eat heavy meals at night in order to sleep and many of them smoked and drank a lot of alcohol to switch off. But it felt inauthentic and it made me feel out of place and alone.

I knew my body was becoming overweight and I felt fat. I was getting pulled into a pattern I knew wasn't in line with my authentic self or the lifting of my vibration. Now to get it clear, I'm not saying that skinnier people have a higher vibration or are more spiritually connected, but I am saying that being more conscious of the physical self and how you fuel it helps you move to higher levels of awareness.

The truth is when you have a strong spiritual practice, you have tools to keep you safe, grounded and focused. When these tools are being used, you won't need to eat foods that are heavy or make you want to sleep in order to switch off.

## Consciously eating

When I started to delve deeply into spirituality, I felt the call to become a vegetarian. I'd read several spiritual books that recommended a vegetarian diet to keep your vibration as high as possible. One of the books suggested that when we consumed animals we were consuming the pain and fear from their death. This produced a haunting image in my mind that has never left me.

I don't believe that we have to be vegetarian to have a high vibration, but it is a personal choice that I believe has supported my path. I have taken it a little bit further, too, by consuming no animal products except for eggs from a local organic chicken-keeper (who does it for a hobby, not profit), and I avoid gluten and wheat products as much as I can.

Eating consciously means eating in a way that you know is causing you, the animal (if you choose to eat meat) and the land the least harm possible. If you are eating meat for example, it means choosing to get it from a sustainable farm that treats the animals in a loving way (or as loving as possible) by allowing them to roam free.

The truth is there are unconscious vegans and vegetarians out there who eat a lot of foods that aren't good for them or the environment. Some people might also be vegan so as not to eat an animal, but at the same time wear leather sandals, for instance, or not recycle their bottles. There's a real call for balance in all of this.

Eating consciously encourages you to go as natural as possible, avoiding genetically modified foods, tinned foods and anything that's been mucked around with. I would recommend going as organic as possible, eating fresh and local when possible and choosing foods that you know make your body happy and healthy.

I remember learning the basics of body messages from a Louise Hay tape. She explained that the body lets you know how energetic food is by how you feel. For example, if you eat something and 20 minutes later you want to go straight to bed and sleep, it's a message loud and clear that your body doesn't like it. Food is a fuel and it's also something you put into the temple that holds your soul. For that reason you want to choose food that has been treated well and is nourishing.

Now I've changed my diet, I feel good when I eat and I feel good about what I eat. I treat myself and eat out often, but always choose places that cater to my needs and make me feel good. I'm well known for leaving restaurants or avoiding buffets or even entire events if they're not going to work for my choice of diet and my body's energy system.

Just recently in Paris I got the hit to leave a restaurant that sold all different kinds of game, including animals that had been hunted that day. It didn't feel in line with my ethos and the truth was I was going to be eating a bare plate of potatoes and salad – which would have been good food, but I wanted to be nourished, not starved. So instead of keeping quiet in order not to disturb the peace of my friends, I was honest and left.

## Blessing your food

Blessing your food is a wonderful way of lifting the energy of what you're about to consume. That way you let the vital life-force in the meal be activated and your body be nourished and supported.

There are several ways you can bless your food. You can visualize it being washed in a golden light, you can imagine light coming from your hands when you place them over it or you can just say a good ol' prayer:

> *'Thank you, universal life-force, for blessing this food with unconditional love. I allow it to nourish every cell of my being!'*

In our home we have love-heart-shaped plates and all our crockery has the word 'Love' stamped onto it – it's a perfect reminder to be mindful at mealtimes.

## Blessing your belly

I realized quite early on my spiritual pathway that it would sometimes be pretty easy to forget blessing my food and it could also be very easy to forget I was eating it. In his book *The Miracle of Mindfulness*, Thich Nhat Hanh explains that mindfulness is awareness of the present moment and what we are doing in it. I know for one that I'm not always mindful – I'll often forget I'm eating something because I'll be emailing at the same time or even texting.

So, when I forget to bless my food, I shift my perceptions by blessing the food in my belly. Sure it might not be in front of me, but it doesn't mean I can't raise the vibration of what I've just eaten.

✦ To bless the food in your belly, place your hands on your belly, close your eyes and breathe towards your hands.

✦ As you do this, imagine that pure divine light is coming from Source (or the universe) to your heart and extending down each arm through your fingers into your belly.

✦ Then say something like:

> *'Thank you, universe, for blessing*
> *the food in my belly! It feels so*
> *good to be nourished and well!'*

## Keeping your body clean and clear

As we've already acknowledged, the body is the temple in which the soul resides and for that reason it's important to keep it radiating and operating at the highest level of vibration we possibly can. There are a few things that I do regularly for my body that I believe keep it working well and keep my energy clean.

## *Salt baths*

Sea salt baths are amazing. For hundreds of years sea salt has been recognized as a sacred tool to clear away anything that is not serving us. I like using pink Himalayan salt in the bath and I've always felt nourished and clear after doing it. I believe it cleanses out the body's energy system and allows the energy centres (the chakras) to express themselves clearly.

All you have to do is put a generous amount of sea salt or pink Himalayan salt in a nice warm bath. I like to put a few drops of my favourite essential oils in the water too in order to add to the luxurious experience.

## *Green juices*

I love a green juice because it's an easy way to nourish the body. Putting fresh organic fruits and vegetables together for a refreshing morning juice is an awesome way to kick-start the day. I believe a healthy gut is important and I've always noticed having a green juice stimulates my digestive system in a healthy way to release and let go.

My favourite recipe for organic green juice is simple: apple, celery, kale, cucumber, carrot, ginger, lemon and spirulina.

## *Colonics*

Probably not the first thing you thought about when I was talking about raising the energy of the body, right? Well, you know that colonic irrigation is all about clearing out your colon? I believe it clears out what you don't need on an energetic level too.

I remember my first experience of colonic hydrotherapy. I didn't expect it to have such a clearing effect on my life. It was as if the room it made on the inside of my digestive system made physical space in my life. I felt more emotionally together and as if a weight had literally been lifted from my body and my energy. I highly recommend visiting a therapist once or twice a year for a good clear-out.

## *Yoga and exercise*

Another great way to raise the energy of the body is through yoga and other forms of exercise. I don't know about you, but once I started to exercise more regularly in a way that pleased me I would leave the class or gym feeling high on life. That feeling of being excited, unstoppable and energized is what's happening to the vibrations we give off too.

If you want to live a high-vibrational lifestyle it's important to find a regular exercise or yoga routine that suits you, your body and your level of fitness. For me, a daily practice of Ashtanga yoga and regular visits to a personal trainer really help me keep my body in shape and my energy high.

# To do list

To look after your body and raise your vibes, do the following:

✦   Check in with your diet and nutrition. Are you eating foods that are making you feel lethargic and drained? How can you improve your existing eating patterns? Are you eating too much or not enough?

+ Begin to bless your food on a regular basis and if you forget, why not try the 'blessing your belly' suggestion I shared above?

+ Add a regular sea salt bath to your spiritual routine – see how it amps up your vibes.

+ Have you tried making a green juice or smoothie at home? If you don't know where to start, your local healthfood store or juice bar is a great place to seek inspiration.

+ If colonics don't speak to you, why not try a detox to kick-start your vibes? Jason Vale's juice detoxes are brilliant!

+ When did you last exercise? How did it make you feel? Find a class that makes your heart sing and your body soar in energy.

# HOW TO USE THIS BOOK

So, now you've learned a bit about energy, the universe has recruited you and you've started raising your vibration, what next?

This part of this book offers 111 different spiritual techniques that will help you lift your energy and keep your vibes high. All of them are easy and accessible. Although some include yoga postures that you can try in order to work on a physical level, most of them can be done anywhere at any time. The 111 lessons are broken into 10 different sections that I'd like to call 'spheres'. Each of these spheres has its own colour scheme, chakra (energy centre) and focus and can help strengthen a particular aspect of your life.

As you progress up the spheres it's as if you're working our way up a spiritual ladder and therefore the lessons will become deeper and more spiritually focused. As you work your way up, you will allow all aspects of your spiritual energy to rise and integrate and eventually activate a higher aspect of yourself.

The purpose of these 111 lessons is to help you move into your own daily spiritual practice. This is essentially the opportunity to acknowledge who you really are. It's the moment when you bring your attention back to yourself and your inner light and choose to turn that light on. That light is needed wherever you are – in the supermarket, on the train, even in the office. And you don't need to go to quiet spaces, temples or the park to turn it on – you can do it anywhere. So, even if a lesson recommends you go somewhere quiet, you don't have to. You might prefer to find a quiet space in which to centre yourself, but it's not a necessity.

Many of the lessons involve meditation. This is a wonderful tool. It's the opportunity to become consciously aware of your mind and your thoughts. Many people feel that they struggle with meditation because they have trouble switching their mind off. The truth is that we'll never be able to silence our mind or our thoughts – and that's not what meditation is really about. It's about being *aware* of our mind and our thoughts. Instead of fighting to eliminate them, it's about taking a step back and being a spectator.

If you ever feel frustrated with your meditation practice, know that the most transformational shift has already happened: that's the fact you've turned up to do it in the first place. Whenever you're choosing to arrive and meditate and listen and go within, you're doing the work.

Another thing to remember is that your vibes are always changing, but the constant and consistent practice of keeping your energy topped up, focusing on the positive and making a conscious effort to change is going to create radical improvements in your life.

# Journey through the chakras

The 111 lessons in this book will take you on a journey through your chakras. If you're not familiar with the chakras, let me help you understand what they are and how the chakra system works.

## *The chakras*

*Chakra* is a Sanskrit word that means 'wheel' and is used to describe an energy centre. The idea is that there are many different energy centres in the body, which are linked to different aspects of body, mind and soul. In traditional yogic teaching there are seven main chakras on a vertical line up the spine, starting at the base and running all the way to the top of the head:

✦ *The root chakra:* This energy centre is the most important of the chakras because in most things you have to start from the ground up. Found at the base of the spine, this space is all about our security and survival but it also represents the health of our legs and back.

✦ *The sacral chakra:* Found just below the navel at the tip of the pubic bone, the sacral chakra governs the reproductive system. This energy space is about our ability to flow with life and express our creativity.

✦ *The solar plexus chakra:* Lying around the centre of the belly, the solar plexus chakra is our 'gut instinct' and is known as the brain of the body. This chakra is all about our willpower and ability to achieve, and governs the digestive system.

✦ *The heart chakra:* At the centre of the chest, this energy centre is all about our capacity to give and receive. It's about love, generosity and being able to share a loving experience. It looks after the heart and upper respiratory system too.

✦ *The throat chakra:* Our ability to communicate, be open and express ourselves is governed by this chakra. Not only does it help us speak our truth but it also has a lot to do with being fully expressive on an emotional level. It looks after the thyroid gland, which is essential for our hormonal stability.

✦ *The brow chakra (the third eye):* The centre of intuition and perception, the brow chakra is concerned with our ability to perceive, on both a physical and non-physical level. It looks after our eyes but helps us develop our inner vision too.

✦ *The crown chakra:* This is the most elevated of the traditional chakras. Some say it's at the crown of the head, while others say it's just above it. This energy centre governs our wisdom and our connection to the divine.

These energy centres are all moving, measuring and experiencing our journey with us. When we are going through challenges in our life, the corresponding chakra(s) can be under pressure. With a daily spiritual practice and a conscious awareness of these centres, however, we can cleanse, balance and energize them.

As well as the traditional chakras, people are now working with newer chakras to create an even stronger connection to divine wisdom. Some say there are nine important chakras, but I'm interested in 10 (seven traditional ones and three newer ones). I mentioned the three additional chakras in my book *Angel Prayers*. They are aspects of the self that we can actualize in our spiritual practice:

✦ *The Earth star chakra:* This chakra is found 15–30 centimetres (6–12 inches) below our feet. It is our connection to the Earth and the wisdom the great mother holds for us. We can use it to anchor ourselves to the heart of the Earth in order to move in harmony with it.

✦ *The soul star chakra:* The soul star, which is seen as a three-dimensional star, sits 15–30 centimetres (6–12 inches) above our crown and we can tap into its energy to awaken deep soul wisdom within us and access the insights of heaven.

✦ *The stellar gateway chakra:* This chakra is so exciting because it represents our ability to connect with the cosmos and bring our hopes and dreams into manifestation. Found around 30 centimetres (12 inches) above the head, it is like a vortex that we can enter in order to be suspended in the heart of the universe.

Although working with the chakras can be subtle, the idea is that it can have an impact on our life. Most spiritual teachings tell us that the outer world is a mirror or expression of what we are experiencing within us. So, my idea is if we can focus on our chakras (which are essentially within us), our outer experience will benefit.

## *Kundalini*

There is also a primal energy found at the base of our spine that's known as *kundalini* and is said to look like a coiled snake. In most of us, this serpent of power is lying dormant, waiting for our spiritual actualization. The Tantras, which are spiritual texts on the practices of some Hindu, Buddhist and Jain sects, teach that when we begin to work with our soul and spiritual energy system this energy will begin to uncoil and move up through our being, helping us reach a deep state of enlightenment. This is essentially what we're doing when we're raising our vibration: we're holding space within ourselves for our primal and most sacred power to unfold.

## *The Sushumna channel*

In order for the kundalini to rise, our chakras have to be connected and activated. This is done through a channel of energy that runs up and down the spine and allows energy to move through the chakras. It is known as *the Sushumna channel*.

Starting at the base chakra, the energy moves up and down the spine while at the same time two streams of energy, known as

*Pingala* (masculine/solar) and *Ida* (feminine/lunar), crisscross each other, creating a vortex of energy every time they cross the Sushumna channel. This essentially creates the chakras. At the crown of the head, all three paths come together as one, allowing the soul self to be fully revealed.

## The lessons and the chakras

Now it's time to begin your journey through the chakras and raise your vibes. Here's how it works:

✦ *Lessons 1–10* take you back to the Earth in search of grounding and stability. This will help you work on your root chakra.

✦ *Lessons 11–20* take you on a journey of flow and expression, which will help you open and connect to your sacral chakra.

✦ *Lessons 21–30* give you the push to ignite your will. They are all about harnessing the power of your solar plexus chakra.

✦ *Lessons 31–40* help you give and receive in a way that's balanced and allow your heart chakra to open and shine.

✦ *Lessons 41–50* encourage you to express yourself in a way that's filled with the purest integrity. This will help your throat chakra to fulfil its ultimate potential.

✦ *Lessons 51–60* help you nourish your inner vision and awaken your third-eye chakra.

✦ *Lessons 61–70* guide you to firm up your connection to the divine and allow your crown chakra to express itself fully.

✦ *Lessons 71–80* encourage you to light up and know that it's safe to be powerful on the planet. This is all about grounding your spiritual tools of support and connecting to the Earth star.

✦ *Lessons 81–90* put into place all the tools to help you manifest the life you love and deserve. Here you let the soul star open and the stellar gateway becomes a vortex of energy to help you create the life of your dreams.

✦ *Lessons 91–100* allow you to harness the power of the cosmos and all the other divine support that's out there. All the chakras are now aligned and ready to guide you to the next expression of your development.

✦ *Lessons 101–111* are about activating all the chakras. There's a sense of repetition here so you can reignite all you have learned through the previous lessons.

## *A lesson a day*

As a dedicated yogi and student of *A Course in Miracles*, I believe that a daily spiritual practice is a wonderful source of support and strength. This is why I recommend that you work through this book by doing a lesson a day and going back to that lesson at various intervals during the day. This will enable you to embody the teaching and allow it to work throughout your life.

I recommend you don't do more than one lesson a day because a spiritual journey can't be rushed – it's not about completing the book, it's about honouring the soul.

## *Oracle lessons*

If you have completed the book and are looking for daily inspiration, you can use it like an oracle. If you would like to know which chakra needs your attention or you would like a spiritual lesson for the day, you can just ask the universe to use the book as its tool and then open a page at random to find your lesson/message of the day.

## *Tips for the journey*

Here are some tips to help you along the way:

✦ Make an appointment with yourself every day to do your lesson. Regularly check in with your lesson.

✦ If you are travelling and can't take the book with you, write the day's principle, teaching, prayer or affirmation down on a piece of paper or take a photo of it on your phone so you can check in with it.

✦ Keep a journal to mark your progress and look back over whatever guidance you have received.

✦ If possible, share your experiences with a friend, meditation teacher or someone who's doing the lessons at the same time as you are.

✦ Be open to new experiences and try not to have any preconceived ideas of what's going to happen.

# GROUND

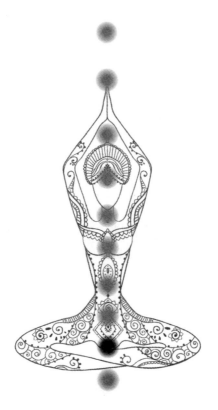

*Chakra:* Muladhara (root)

*Location:* The base of the spine

*Colour:* Red

*Element:* Earth

*Muladhara* is a Sanskrit word that means 'root support'. It's the name of the spiritual energy centre that represents our connection to the Earth and our sense of groundedness in life. If the root chakra were in nature, it would be the soil in which seeds are planted. It's the chakra that is linked to our ability to survive and stay grounded and upright in life.

The parts of the body related to this chakra are the legs and feet and the base of the spine. This chakra holds us up and is the base from which the other chakras move upwards.

Here is where you start with the foundational practices that are going to support your growth and raise your vibration. In the lessons that follow you will reconnect to the Earth through affirmations, posture and prayer. The theory is that if you have a sense of connection to where you are now, you allow the spiritual energy within you to rise, which in turn will lift and strengthen your connection to the cosmos.

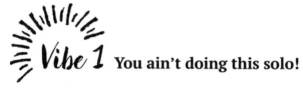 **Vibe 1** You ain't doing this solo!

Everything in the universe is energy, including you. For that reason, you don't walk this path alone. You are connected to everyone and everything that is, was and ever will be. You are connected to the essence of life because it's moving through every aspect of your being.

The moment you are born you are given the gift of free will. Although as a child you don't fully understand it, you can still decide when you want food and even when you want support. Your free will really starts to unfold as you develop and it's put into full use when you enter adult life. You get to decide what you want to do, who you want to do it with and when and where you do it. You are essentially in control.

The same goes for support. The universe has given us the chance to decide how we walk this path, and although it would love to help us, it can't do so unless we choose to ask. Many people live their lives feeling unsupported and alone – they generally don't realize that just a shift in perception can change that.

Independence is seen as strength on Earth. Being able to do your own thing and not ask for help seems to be positive. The downside is that many people feel it is 'weak' to ask for help. In spirituality we honour independence, but we also note that there is another option: co-creation.

In order to raise your vibration and move beyond the limited thoughts that can make you feel isolated, you have to surrender the idea of being independent and move into the space of co-creating with the creator. (Your vision of the creator will be different from mine and it can be 'God' or it can just be 'life', but whatever works for you is right.)

Today, realize that you are walking this path with your creator, with the universe and with the energy you are co-creating. When you realize that you don't have to do everything on your own, a huge weight is lifted from your shoulders. Essentially you are allowing the weight of your own world to be held by a power that is greater than you are.

# Vibe of the day

*Here's today's vibe. This is all about intention. There's no right or wrong way to get this intention running for you. Maybe meditate on it, say it, pray it or dance it. If the intention is right, the vibe is right!*

*'Today I choose to surrender my independence.*

*I choose to remember that I don't walk this path alone.*

*I am co-creating my world with my creator.*

*Angels dance around me.*

*As everything in the universe is made of energy, including me, I choose to welcome the energy of support and love into my life.*

*Today I choose to walk with the universe, knowing it's supporting every step I take.'*

# #ShareYourVibe
*'I accept that I am fully supported by the universe.'*

# Vibe 2 This world is blessed to have you!

When we grow up in this world there's a lot going on that can make us feel very small. So part of us is trained to be modest. If we brush past someone for example, we'll say 'Sorry.' This can be seen as good manners, but have you ever felt that you're saying that word too much? If your answer is 'yes', it's important to access the inner story that's going on. Are you looking to be excused for existing? Do you feel that you have a right to be here on Earth?

You are an essential part of this world and it's important that you know it. In fact it's important that you *own* it. You have a divine right to be here and the universe is grateful that you are.

Are you surprised to hear that? Do you feel that you're creating more challenges and problems down here than you'd like? If so, there's a great chance that your inner story is 10 times harsher than reality.

In order to raise your vibration today you must accept that you have a right to be here and recognize that you are a beautiful facet of this world. The fact that you are here is a gift in itself and anything that you bring with you is a bonus.

You don't need an excuse for your presence. You don't have to take on a heap of responsibility to justify your existence either. That's just your ego talking.

The fact that you are here today is a gift to the world. Believe it.

## Vibe of the day

*'I have a right to be here on Earth.*

*I choose to let go of the need to excuse my presence.*

*My presence alone is my purpose; everything else is a bonus.*

*It feels so good to know that I am a facet of the greater picture.*

*I accept that it is my divine right to be alive
and I am so grateful for this gift.'*

### #ShareYourVibe
*'I am so grateful to be here on Earth!'*

## Vibe 3 Right now is a gift – that's why it's called the present!

There is no place more powerful than the present moment. This very moment is when you are at your most powerful. But most of us choose to think about our past or what we need to do next.

Today's technique is all about getting back to the present moment. Imagine for a moment that there's a beautiful golden light above your head and it's moving to the tips of your fingers and toes. The same golden light is moving over and through every cell of your skin. It is moving through your vital organs and through the air you breathe. It is replenishing your lungs and dancing through the flow of your blood.

The light that you are imagining is life itself and essentially it's made of love. On a subtle level right now it's moving through us all, but because we are so busy with what's going on in our lives we forget about this beautiful connection to the universe.

When you choose to remember this light and to breathe with ease, knowing you are part of it, you recognize the gift of life. And when you recognize the gift of life, you raise your vibration so high that you can ignite a light in other people.

When you welcome miracles and gifts into your life, you don't deprive others of them. In fact, by recognizing the beauty of the universe, accepting its support and feeling grateful for it, you are demonstrating to others how they can feel supported too.

Today, up your vibes by recognizing that raising your vibration is not only a gift you give to yourself but a gift you offer to others simply through your smile.

## Vibe of the day

*'I choose to breathe with ease, knowing that life is present with me now.*

*Knowing I am connected to the presence of life makes me feel safe and alive.*

*I offer the presence of the present to others through my smile today.*

*I smile, knowing that life is smiling upon
and through me.*

*My presence is a gift.'*

# #ShareYourVibe
*'I offer the gift of the present to others through my smile.'*

# Vibe 4 **You are safe**

Feeling safe is essential to raising your vibration. Increasing your positive frequency involves opening your heart, and to do that you must cultivate a space within you that feels safe.

I for one know what it feels like to be vulnerable. In my teens I was overwhelmed by anxiety after being chased by a gang of youths one night while walking home from a friend's house. I was just taking my usual route home when all of a sudden a huge gang turned the corner and starting coming towards me at quite the pace. I could hear them shouting and sense the violent energy coming from them. Instantly my body wanted to run and before I knew it I was bolting down the street. Turning to peek back, I noticed that they were running now too. I raced through the security door of my apartment block and felt secure at last – but they still tried to get in by kicking the door.

After that episode I felt vulnerable all through my teens when I was walking the streets. It was only later in life that I learned that my focus was encouraging this. I believed that I could be attacked and couldn't get that out of my mind. I really believe that's why I had experiences like that growing up.

At the same time, the incident with the youths can be used as a metaphor. What do I mean by this? The gang can be seen to represent my fearful thoughts. And if I keep running from them, I'll never escape them – they'll always be there in my mind. If I believe they can hold me back then of course they will.

So, in order to move into a safe place, we all have to acknowledge the fears we have and in all honesty we have to 'feel them out', gaze right into them and recognize them for what they are.

Fears are not real. They are figments of our imagination or memories of our past playing over and over again. They can really bring us down. But experiencing fear is an opportunity to move into the space of fearlessness.

I've found that the medicine for overcoming my own fears is the idea that I can never really be hurt. You see, within us there is an amazing light and it's called the soul. It's the part of us that is eternal and it can never be hurt, damaged or tarnished.

When we trust that we're unbreakable, we will create experiences in our life that will reflect our feeling of safety.

## Vibe of the day

'There is no place safer for me to be than in my body.

My body is the home of my soul.

My outer self is a reflection of my inner self.

My soul is the true and real aspect of me and it can never be broken, tarnished or damaged.

My soul is healed and whole.

*Today I claim my safety, because the light of my
soul shines within a light of protection.*

*I am safe!'*

**#ShareYourVibe**
*'I am safe in my body because it is the home of my soul.'*

# Vibe 5 Thank your earthly mama!

I had a bumper sticker on my first car. It read: 'The Earth is our mother, treat her with respect.'

We are so blessed to be on this Earth and to be experiencing this life. The Earth is a wonderful place to be. What's going wrong on this planet hasn't anything to do with Mother Nature – it has everything to do with us. Every day when I get onto my yoga mat I like to give thanks to the Earth and tune in to her rhythm.

When we begin to raise our vibration, we also help to raise the frequency of the planet. The more spiritually aware we become, the more conscious of the Earth we become and the more we look after the planet.

If we are littering the street or avoiding doing the recycling then we aren't exactly coming from a place that's heart-centred. If we are helping nature, looking after her, giving thanks for her and doing our best to keep our part of the world clean then we are also keeping it spiritually clean, and that means we can hold more space for light there.

While you are on this journey, ask yourself what you can do to help Mother Earth. Can you feed her birds? Clean the local park, beach or forest? Can you use less plastic or contribute more to your recycling? All of these steps help you become more aware of the world that surrounds you and help you clean up your inner world too.

# Vibe of the day

Today, give thanks to Mother Earth. How can you do it? I'm going to introduce you to the yoga pose I do while giving thanks. It's suitable for all levels of fitness and I really believe it helps me become one with the great mother. It's called *Balasana*, or Child's Pose (extended version). You can do it at home or even somewhere in nature that you love.

✦ Come onto your knees and spread them about hip-width apart (or as wide as your yoga mat if you have one), while keeping your big toes touching.

✦ Then lean forwards and bring your forehead and hands to the ground in front of you.

✦ Allow your fingers to spread wide as your palms press down into the Earth.

✦ With every out-breath, allow your hips to sink deep down towards your heels, giving your spine a beautiful stretch.

Balasana: *Child's pose*

You can use this prayer or share your own:

*'Mother Earth,*

*I am your child. Thank you for being here. It feels so good to be here on this planet. Today I vow to do my very best to help you along in your evolution. I know that as you grow and evolve I will too.*

*Thank you for all of your blessings to this point in my life. I feel very blessed.'*

#ShareYourVibe
*'Today I choose to honour the Earth because she is our mother!'*

# Vibe 6 Abundance is a state of mind

Today you are encouraged to see the riches in your life – and not just the material ones. We have a tendency to measure how rich we are by the things we have and the certificates on our wall. When we do this, though, we are measuring our own worth and there's a danger that we will never feel good enough.

The universe doesn't measure us at all. As far as it's concerned, we are all perfect because within us there's a perfect spark of splendour – an extension of divine love itself.

You may not feel perfect, or rich, but you are richer than you think. What blessings do you have? What gifts do you have?

Everything you 'have' on this Earth is just an external representation of how rich you feel within. You can never be rich if you feel poor, so it's time to feel rich again.

Abundance is a state of mind. Today give thanks for the people, places, blessings and gifts in your life and let your soul feel rich.

# Vibe of the day

Spend time going through some of the aspects of your life that you are grateful for and say:

*'I am grateful to be here and I am grateful to be a spark of splendour in this world.*

*Today I recognize that my life is full of abundance and fulfilment in so many ways.*

*I am rich because I am a soul filled with divine light.*

*I allow this light to shine through my entire day and my entire life.*

*It feels so good to be this blessed.'*

# #ShareYourVibe
*'My world is a reflection of my inner riches and it is full of abundance.'*

# Vibe 7 It's cool to be kind, baby!

The spiritual law of attraction is simple. It teaches that whatever we believe to be true is what we're going to experience in the world. It's really important to bring this ancient and sacred teaching into your awareness so that you can cultivate a mindset that is working *for* you, not against you.

Your inner dialogue has a lot to do with your beliefs and how you experience the world. Are the conversations in your mind mostly loving? Or are there loads of fears floating around?

It's okay to have fears floating around, but it's also important to know that your natural state – the greatest part of you – is love.

In honouring the natural loving state that is somewhere within you today, you are encouraged to have kind conversations with yourself. How you see and speak to yourself in the mirror has a lot to do with the beliefs that you have. So today, go to your mirror and find out what starts to happen there. Do you start criticizing what you see and who you are? How can you change your inner conversation to be more loving? How can you be kinder to yourself?

As you already know, your body is the home of your soul. It's the temple that is holding your divine light, so why not honour that and speak to yourself in a kind way?

If you begin to chat lovingly to yourself but find that your ego self (that inner critic) puts up a fight, be kind to them too. Say, 'Thanks for sharing, but today I choose kindness.'

When you are kind to yourself, it allows your energy to be open to kindness on all levels. You give those you love an easier time and they give you an easier time too. Your kindness to yourself is a prayer of kindness to the world. And you're setting an example for those around you and the generations that will follow.

# Vibe of the day

*'Today I choose to be kind to myself.*

*Today I choose to honour my soul.*

*Today I recognize that my natural state is good.*

*I allow all false thoughts and criticisms to fade away.*

*My kindness is a prayer to the divine within and the divine in others.*

*I allow kindness to flow through all areas in my life.'*

### #ShareYourVibe

*'My kindness is a prayer to and demonstration of the natural goodness that is within us all.'*

# Vibe 8 Keep calm and co-operate

Sometimes it can be very easy to be pulled into the mindset that life is working against you, but it's not! The universe is always working in accordance with your free will. It wants you to be happy, abundant and fulfilled. It loves you more than words can describe. Let it support you.

Today you are invited to co-operate with the universe by keeping calm. If something has gone 'wrong', know that the universe has a greater plan. Instead of having a meltdown or freaking out, keep calm. Remember the field of energy that surrounds you and moves through you responds to every thought, feeling and intention you have. If you feel that it's not working with you and that there's some sort of karma trail following you, well, that's what you'll experience.

So, today, choose to know that you are being supported, held and led by the presence of light that exists within you. Take several deep breaths and trust that the universe will co-operate with you when you co-operate with it. You are a team. Know it is your biggest fan, your greatest supporter and the cheerleader of your soul.

## Vibe of the day

*'The universe is my greatest supporter.*
*Today I choose to co-operate and keep calm.*
*The power that created me is always working in my favour.*
*This I know and trust.'*

### #ShareYourVibe
*'The universe is my soul's greatest cheerleader.'*

## Vibe 9 Rock your root chakra!

Your root chakra, Muladhara, is one of the seven major spiritual centres in your body. It's at the base of your spine and represents your stability, security, connection to the Earth and your loved ones, and your ability to stand strong in life. It's known to be red – the foundational colour of focus and strength.

Our chakras are our spiritual anatomy: they govern our acceleration to the divine. When they are balanced, we experience a deeper connection to ourselves and to our inner guidance. When the root chakra is over-energized, we can become over-attached to the physical world and everything in it and overly rely on having certain comforts, people or things around us. Although it's cool to have things that make us feel comfortable, when we get over-attached to things, or people, we lose our inner power.

The root chakra can also become depleted. This can happen very easily, especially if too many people rely on us or there is pressure in our life, and it can make us feel that there's lack in our life, that there's not enough for everyone and even that we aren't safe. On a physical level, if our root chakra is depleted we can have major lower-back issues and our finances can crumble before our eyes.

It's always good to keep track of your root chakra and up its energy when needed. Try the following visualization.

## Vibe of the day

✦ Place your hands, right on top of left, flat on the space just below your pubic bone. Breathe into them.

✦ Imagine that there is a nicely sized cone of red light coming from your tailbone and swirling underneath your hands. Then say:

> *'I am at peace with myself.*
> *I am at peace with my body.*
> *I am at peace with the Earth.*

*I am safe because of my soul.*

*I am unbound because of my strength.*

*I am strongly rooted to the Earth.*

*I completely accept that I have
everything I need within me.*

*It is my spiritual right to be connected to myself.*

*I am grounded, focused and free.'*

✦ Breathe/meditate for as long as you need.

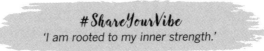

**#ShareYourVibe**
*'I am rooted to my inner strength.'*

# Vibe 10 Turn your frown upside down

Everything you do in this world moves out from you like a wave of energy. When you are kind, happy and harmonious, this wave extends to all those who cross your pathway. And the kindness you share is eventually going to come back to you.

People always say, 'What comes around, goes around!' and I know they like to drop the word 'karma' online, especially if someone has been challenging in their life, but that's not the point. Karma, the law of cause and effect, is ultimately a spiritual tool to encourage us to be kind and loving.

When you are kind to others, you are literally being kind to yourself too. When you focus on what makes you happy it's as if the doors of your heart swing open and you move into the space of love that rests gently within. When you experience this love, you welcome all those around you into this space too. So, every time you experience bliss and joy you are literally holding the space for others to experience it too. Your happiness is a wave of healing to the whole world.

Today you are encouraged to recognize all the simple things that make you feel happy. When you are happy, you raise your vibration to the divine and you allow others to raise their vibration too. Happiness is infectious. Think of it – when someone starts to smile, you can't take that smile off your face either, can you?

Today's exercise is smiling as much as you can. Offer the gift of joy to all those you meet. Everywhere you go, look for the simple blessings that surround us all.

Today, recognize that happiness is a gift and it's yours anytime you allow it to be.

## Vibe of the day

*'Happiness is a gift.*
*I am blessed with joy.*
*Every smile I share allows this gift to be shared.*
*Today I recognize the blessings in my world.'*

### #ShareYourVibe
*'My happiness sends healing to the world.'*

# FLOW

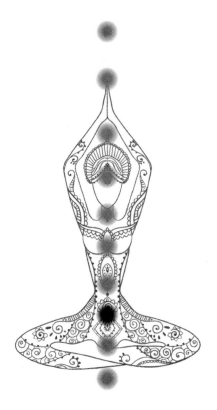

*Chakra:* Svadhisthana (sacral)

*Location:* Between the genitals and the pubic bone

*Colour:* Orange

*Element:* Water

*Svadhisthana* is a Sanskrit word meaning 'one's own place'. It is the name of the spiritual energy centre that governs every aspect of creativity, including creating life on Earth. If the sacral chakra were in nature, it would be the water replenishing the soil and allowing the seeds to germinate and grow.

The parts of the body related to this chakra are the genitalia and lower abdomen. This centre governs the reproductive system and the ability to bring life to the Earth.

Here you begin to step into the flow of your world, connect to the element of water and make space inside yourself to honour the more sacred aspects of your being. In the following lessons you'll be delving into your emotions and creativity and taking time to give credit to your sexual organs.

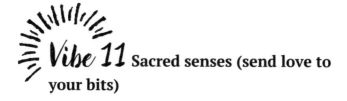

# *Vibe 11* Sacred senses (send love to your bits)

The sacral chakra is the sacred space that is related to our reproductive organs and for that reason it represents our ability to create. We can create life from this centre. What else can we create?

In order to raise your vibration today, you are encouraged to look at your reproductive organs (yes, your genitals) in a loving way. A great deal of shame is held within the genitals and that needs to change. Somewhere along the line we've lost our sense of loving and belonging to our genitalia and right now is the time to find it again. These amazing body parts allow us to bring life into this world and to make love to our partner in life. They are sacred, divine and, as far as the universe is concerned, they are the space in which we create.

Today you are encouraged to send love from your heart to your genitals. Thank them silently for playing their divine part in your life.

When you acknowledge this sacred centre of creation as beautiful, you come into special alignment with your inner creativity – and this is the part of you that manifests positivity in your life!

## Vibe of the day

+ With your eyes open or closed, imagine an amazing light streaming from your heart centre to your genitals. Imagine them being washed in a golden light of unconditional love.

+ Then give thanks to them for being the special instruments they are. Say:

*'Today I honour the sacredness of my body.*
*My sexual organs are a gift and I am grateful for them.*
*I have the light of creation within me today.*
*I allow myself to flow freely, expressing who I am.'*

#ShareYourVibe
*'I welcome freedom through the honouring of my sacred self.'*

## Vibe 12 Embody your body!

Have you noticed that it has become popular and even on trend to be busy? We go around with full schedules and have grown used to being on the go.

There's nothing wrong with being busy, but sometimes when we get pulled into the vortex of activity we forget about our own needs and can miss a lot of the messages our body and soul are sending us.

Have you allowed yourself to become addicted to being busy? Do you feel lost when your schedule for the day is empty? If the answer is 'yes', it's time to change that.

Have you ever noticed that if you've had a really busy few months, when you finally take a holiday or even a day off, you get sick? That's your body making sure that you finally stop and just take some time to be with yourself.

When you come back to your body, you come back to the clearest guidance system you have. When you give yourself the amazing gift of more time to really listen, you'll hear what the body wants you to know. If you take the time to check in with your body on a regular basis, you won't have to face a more intense signal from it when it needs your attention.

Today you are encouraged to come back into your body. Take some time to give thanks for this amazing vehicle and the messages it sends you. Your body wants nothing more than to be happy and healthy, and if you really, really listen to it, it will tell you what it needs in order to be well.

You can even ask your body if it would like certain types of food or drink. All you have to do is close your eyes, come back to your breath, think of the particular food or drink and ask, 'Is this what you would like today?' or 'Will this agree with you today?' You will instinctively get a clear feeling of 'yes' or 'no'.

When you become more aware of the natural rhythms and messages of your body, you will become spiritually 'embodied', and this deeper state of awareness will allow you to raise your vibration.

Your body is the home of your soul. Listen to it and learn how it can support you on your spiritual pathway.

# Vibe of the day

✦ Closing your eyes and taking a few deep breaths, just become aware of your body and the natural flow of your breath.

✦ Instinctively place your hands on a part of your body that you feel needs your attention or some more energy.

✦ Breathe deeply into your hands and allow your breath to carry extra life-force energy to this area of your body.

✦ Listen to anything you feel your body wants you to know. Become aware of the natural signs, signals and messages it sends you.

✦ When you're ready, set your intention with the words:

*'Today I choose to arrive within my body.*

*It feels so good to be connected to the natural messages my body sends me.*

*Every cell of my being is blessed today because I am in touch with a deeper part of myself.*

*I am so grateful for the chance to know when my body needs my attention and love.*

*Every breath I take restores me in every way that's right for me.*

*I am embodied, connected and in touch with who I truly am.'*

# #ShareYourVibe
*'My body always tells me what it needs.'*

# *Vibe 13* Sensitivity is so special

In our world, expressing emotion has never really been encouraged. You just have to look at an average parent with a child who has just hurt themselves: 'Shhhh,' they'll say as they rub the child's sore bruise, or even, 'Stop crying, come on.'

Did your parents display emotion or not? Did you ever see your mum cry or did she say, 'I'm fine,' and try to hide it if she was upset? Did your dad hold his emotions in? It's highly likely. From very early on in our lives, we learn that being emotional is wrong.

The truth is, emotions are a gift. They are messages from our body and heart telling us something is important. If we ignore them, we are ignoring any guidance that is coming through.

When you raise your vibration, you begin to trust your emotions, and the insights the universe is bringing you will be as clear as day.

Today you are encouraged to observe your emotions. What are they? How can you express them?

When you really allow yourself to express your emotions, you give yourself an opportunity to pick up the messages that are coming through to you on an intuitive level.

True emotions are beautiful and it's okay to be sensitive.

## Vibe of the day

*'Emotions are messengers of the soul.*
*It is okay for me to feel them.*

*Acknowledging how I feel allows me to*
*open up to the voice of spirit.*

*My intuition speaks to me through my emotions.*

*Today I claim my emotions and allow*
*them to flow freely through me.*

*It's safe to express them.'*

### #ShareYourVibe

*'My emotions are the messengers of my*
*soul. I wholly embrace them.'*

## *Vibe 14* Forget about fashion – follow your passion!

We are so blessed to be in this world because there are unlimited opportunities for us to learn and grow. The beauty of this world is the fact that we are all different and we all have our own interests. We all have something that we are passionate about.

Passion is a natural energy that flows through all of us. It helps us express who we really are and share our gifts, talents and creativity with the world.

Our passion can be something to do with our career or a hobby that we are involved in. As I mentioned earlier, I love practising yoga and I love snowboarding. I feel uplifted every time I do either of these activities. When I feel that rush of excitement and fulfilment, all ideas of lack or limitation leave my mind and I feel full and supported.

Our truest form – our soul – is always in a place that is filled with support, abundance and fulfilment. When we do what we love, we allow that sense of abundance to move into our body and mind – we experience it on a physical level.

What's your passion? What do you love to do? When you choose to do what you love, you express yourself fully and become centred with your soul.

Your passion is prosperous too. When you let go of what you think you should do and follow what you instinctively feel is right for you, all limitations in your mind begin to melt away. When you're in a place of deep excitement and love, you're lifted so high on a vibrational level that you're in touch with the totality of possibility and you move onto a frequency that has unlimited support and potential for you. If you believe that you have the ability to create positive changes in your life, this is the time to do it, my friend. When you are pulsing within your passion you are literally within the heart of the universe and you can manifest the life you love.

# Vibe of the day

Today you are encouraged to find some time, even if it's 10 minutes, to do what you love or, if that's really not possible, to *dream* about what you love. It's important that this is done without pressure or expectation, so choose something that's not connected with your work.

When you are doing (or dreaming of) what you love, really feel the excitement. Enjoy every moment and breathe it all in.

Then, if you have any goals or dreams of manifesting something in your life, hold them in your mind and say:

> 'It feels so good to do what I love.
>
> When I experience my passion in life, I am unbound and limitless.
>
> My passion is a form of prosperity and it
> feels so good to be prosperous!
>
> I move into the totality of possibility that surrounds me.
>
> It feels so good to experience more of what I love in my daily life!
>
> And so it is!'

**#ShareYourVibe**
'Experiencing my passions is
experiencing prosperity.'

# Vibe 15 Keep your relationships real!

When you start to raise your vibration, you have a greater idea of who you are, what you have to offer and what you'd like to experience on your path. This brings so much clarity to the relationships you have in your life.

The deeper your spiritual exploration, the deeper your need will be for honest relationships. It's important to know that in a spiritual sense, no relationship in your life is wrong. Every person you meet on your pathway offers you the perfect opportunity to connect to the divine.

If there are people in your life you aren't fully resonating with, though, that's okay. Don't feel guilty for not being on the same page as them. In spiritual circles, when two people don't get on, one person always says something like 'And you're supposed to be so spiritual!' It's important to know that not seeing eye to eye with someone doesn't make you (or them) any more or less spiritual.

When you realize a relationship in your life isn't congruent with the rest of your path and you don't want to be associated with that person any more, you are listening to your soul. When you decide to let go of that relationship, you are honouring divine guidance.

Instead of feeling used or abused, just be honest with yourself and the person involved. When you offer someone the gift of honesty, you take the weight of the world off your own shoulders and you offer the other person the gift of freedom.

If there's a relationship that you are ready to let go, work on the most compassionate and appreciative way of doing that. Send the person love and gratitude for the relationship to this point. Then imagine you are cutting all of the fearful and limiting cords that are holding you both back.

In order to be more in your flow and to experience uplifting and fulfilling relationships, first of all be honest with yourself. What are you looking for? Then, if you are ready to find your tribe or form a friendship with someone who is coming from the same space you're in, think about how you can make room for it in your life. If you love a particular hobby and would like a friend to join you in it, can you join a group of enthusiasts and be open to speaking to new people? Can you send your thoughts out to the universe? Imagine yourself surrounded by people who are like-minded and friendly – just like you.

Give thanks for the relationships you love. Tell the people involved what you love about them, ask how you can support them and be real in your gratitude for the positive and honest connection you have.

# Vibe of the day

Today you are encouraged to honour the honesty of your relationships by being grateful for the people in your life and the good times you have shared.

If you're feeling challenged by a relationship that's important to you, it's essential to highlight its strengths rather than its weaknesses in order to move forwards in a high-vibrational way.

✦ Close your eyes and think about the relationships that have touched your life.

✦ Give thanks for the close ones and really imagine them being blessed with ultimate happiness. Then say:

*'All of the relationships in my life reflect honesty.*

*I am grateful for the people who love me.*

*It feels so good to know that I am clear in my relationships and that I support and feel supported in perfect balance.*

*Every relationship in my world is a divinely guided relationship.*

*Today I recognize the divine in myself and others.'*

### #ShareYourVibe
*'Every relationship is an opportunity to experience the divine.'*

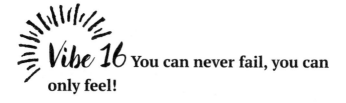

# Vibe 16 You can never fail, you can only feel!

The word 'failure' is something we never like to hear. It's something we fear and want to avoid. But 'failure' is an illusion that the external world has created for us – and we decide whether we fall into that nightmare or not.

According to spiritual law, we can never really fail. Our energy is unlimited because the universe is unlimited and *we are the universe*.

Today you are going to tackle the old idea of failure so that you can surmount it once and for all.

In order to move beyond a limiting belief like failure, you have to understand how it's created in the first place. The truth is that failure is just one person's opinion with regard to the outcome of a situation. When we say something is 'a failure' or 'we've failed', we're basically saying that something didn't turn out according to plan or the way we hoped.

What if I were to suggest to you that 'failure' was just the universe having a different plan? What if, when something goes 'wrong', there's a bigger picture there? What if there's a better opportunity coming in your direction and if things had gone according to plan you would have missed it?

Today you are encouraged to surrender your expectations. It's time to realize you can't actually let down the universe because the universe has no expectations of you in the first place. You are encouraged to realize that failure is just a feeling and that feeling is simply the acknowledgement that things didn't go the way you wanted. It doesn't mean things aren't going to be good.

Failure can only exist for people who want control. So, to overcome the idea of failure, you are encouraged to surrender the idea of control.

It's time to realize that whatever you focus on, whether good or bad, you are sending energy to it. When you fear failure, you are setting yourself up for it. When you're surrendering to the universe, to that ultimate force of goodness, you're setting yourself up to experience goodness.

It's time to come into the awareness that when your plans go wrong, the universe has a greater plan. That's all. It wants you to know that no external achievement will ever determine how amazing you are and it wants you to trust that it's always working for your greatest good.

You are reminded that you can never stray from your path to growth. You can never fail at being who you are. Every experience in your life is a perfect opportunity to know yourself at a deeper level.

# Vibe of the day

*'Today I realize that no external experience or achievement can determine my self-worth.*

*My only truth is that I am an expression of the divine.*

*As I am an expression of the divine, I am a being of unconditional love.*

*I accept that I am always doing the best I can.*

*I honour myself and my journey. I recognize how far I have come and I am enjoying the view right now.*

*Today I know that I haven't lost my way because I have found myself.'*

#ShareYourVibe
*'No experience or achievement can determine my worth because love cannot be measured.'*

# Vibe 17 Accept that you are awesome

In order to live a fuller life and feel comfortable with who you are, you need to accept your awesomeness. The fact that you are here on Earth in the first place is amazing, but really you need to consider the idea that you are a walking, talking miracle!

You are a soul in a body, and because of that, infinite potential moves through you. You are a limitless being, but you are in a world which creates limits. How can you deal with that?

Know that when you feel you are up against limits and are frustrated or annoyed with someone (or yourself), you are doing yourself no favours. When you have regrets and live a life filled with shoulda, woulda, coulda, you are limiting your whole earthly experience. When you constantly think about your past, you just end up recreating your own history instead of moving forwards. Every time you experience the feeling of being held back by the world, *you must remember that you are a being of brilliant potential*.

Your true self has no cruelty within it. Your true self is always healed and complete. It's only the ego, the limiting thinking mind, that wants you to limit yourself through self-sabotage and causing harm to others.

Acceptance is the spiritual art of acknowledging your true self. It's the moment when you decide to let go of fear and allow love to be your guide. When you accept yourself, blame, judgement and anger aren't important any more. When you accept everyone and everything exactly as they are, you feel uplifted, empowered and whole.

When you accept that you are a mighty incredible, supremely spiritual being, you embrace the truth of who you are. And you are awesome!

# Vibe of the day

Ask yourself the following questions. Between each one, close your eyes and breathe. Really feel your soul's response to what you are asking.

*'How good would it feel to be accepted?'*

*'What can I do to accept myself more?'*

*'How can I embrace my past so I can experience my present?'*

Then set your intention as follows:

*'Today I choose to accept myself and the world.*

*I decide to move beyond thoughts that have limited me in the past.*

*I release all actions and experiences that were cruel.*

*I recognize that my true self is love.*

*My true self is luminous. My true self is filled with light. My true self is real.*

*Today I accept who I am: a soul, an expression of love and an important part of the world.'*

### #ShareYourVibe
*'I accept the wholeness of my soul.'*

# Vibe 18 Have a date with your desires

'Desire' is a powerful word. It's an intense, fluid and exciting word. It's not just a word – it's a feeling, a sense of longing for something, someone, even a fantasy. In the past we have all dropped our desires and left them by the wayside, but today that changes.

The most important thing for you to know right now is that you are allowed to have desires, you are allowed to have cravings and you are allowed to experience those desires and cravings.

We all want to get somewhere in life, to reach our goals. It's okay to want things and it's okay to strive for something – especially if you're on the highest road possible.

When you have a desire for something, it's best to check it's a healthy desire, though. So, first of all, ask yourself why you want it. If it's because it's going to make you happy or a better person, that's cool! The truth is that no thing or situation can make you any more divine than you already are, but you're allowed to enjoy this world and the things that are in it. Just breathe with that for a moment – you're allowed to have desires!

Most people don't allow themselves to have desires because they feel they're being selfish. It's almost as though at some deep level they believe that if they have something, particularly something luxurious or expensive, they're depriving someone else of it. But in receiving something, we're actually bringing balance to the world.

Many of us feel that we're constantly giving in life. We can feel that we're giving so much of ourselves that there's nothing else to give.

When we're receiving, the first thing that's happening is that we're redressing the balance. The second thing is that we're teaching those around us that they too can receive.

The universe is happy to share its energy with us. And that energy never ceases to be, never runs out and can never die. There is more than enough energy in the universe for everyone and that energy is the creator of all things. Today, realize that there is no lack in the heart of the creator and there is no need to have lack in your life.

When you decide to honour your desires, you give yourself permission to dance with the universe and receive support for your growth and happiness.

# Vibe of the day

You are encouraged to have a date with your desires today.

✦  What is it you want in life?

✦  How will it make you feel when those desires are met?

✦  What can you do to create that feeling now?

✦  How can you express that emotion?

✦  Do it!

Here's today's intention:

*'Desire is a powerful emotion.*

*I have recognized that I have needs and
I am finally honouring them.*

*It's okay for me to want some things from life because
the truth is there's enough for everyone.*

*In receiving, I bring balance to the world.*

*In manifesting, I show others that they can manifest too.*

*I am grateful to be held by the universe as it
meets my needs for the highest good of all.'*

# #ShareYourVibe
'Today I have a date with my
desires and it feels so good!'

# Vibe 19 Divine dance party!

I've always been up for a wee dance. I absolutely love having
a shimmy and a shake to my favourite music. One thing that's
always supported me in a 'solo' dance-off is the idea that when I'm
dancing, angels are dancing all around me.

When we move our hips from side to side and twirl, swirl and
shake, we're essentially moving into the flow of life. When we dance
to our favourite music and really let loose, we let go of our fears
and cares for those few minutes and on a spiritual level we express
our soul through movement.

I've always believed in the idea of 'victory dancing'. Victory dancing
is all about manifestation. The idea is to think about your desires,
your goals and your dreams and feel that the universe has already
delivered them into your life. As you get high on the idea of receiving
these gifts, you dance – and create the energy for them to be real.
It's as though your movement helps you harness the strength and
support of the universe in physical form.

Victory dancing is something I do regularly on stage at my events and I spoke about it in my book *Angel Prayers*. When we do it, we're essentially raising our vibes because we're moving into a state of joy. And when our vibes are high, we can receive guidance and blessings and manifest our heart's desire.

When was the last time you had a dance to your favourite song? Did you realize it was a spiritual practice?

# Vibe of the day

Today you are encouraged to have a divine dance party. Clear your space and clear your vibes through the power of movement. It doesn't matter what time of day it is and it definitely doesn't matter what your choice of music is, just ensure it's high energy and filled with joy.

Think about your heart's desire, say your prayers silently or out loud, imagine your wildest of dreams being fulfilled or visualize yourself overcoming a challenge you're working on. Feel light fill your being and allow it to radiate from your aura. Then whack on your favourite track and celebrate as if the universe has already met your needs.

Here's your intention:

'Today I have danced with the universe.

My expression through movement
is an expression of my soul.

Angels swirl with joy around me.

I have recognized that there is an unlimited
presence of light within me.

I share my light with the world through my joy!'

# *Vibe 20* Flowing and glowing!

The last 10 lessons have been about accepting and expressing ourselves and, in the process, honouring and energizing our sacral chakra. This space is sacred because it allows us to create life and for that reason it's closely associated with abundance. It's even more exciting that the sacral centre is also the water centre of the body – and water is the element that supports abundance. The way I like to explain it is that the universe has a massive pool of energy and it's waiting for us to draw it into our life.

That means you too: you are entitled to abundance, support and energy in your life. The universe is just standing by for you to take full advantage of what it has to offer. All the way through this section of the book we've recognized that there is more than enough for everyone. Today, accept your 'enoughness'.

## Vibe of the day

Today's lesson is a little bit different from some of the others because we're going to practise a yoga pose with movement and breath. This pose is all about strengthening our sacral centre. We're drawing down the energy of abundance from the unlimited pool that the universe holds, and to top it all off, this is a great pose for toning the legs and butt!

The pose we are doing today is called Goddess, or *Utkata Konasana*, which translates as 'Fierce Angle Pose'. We are going to do it with open arms, open palms, which represents being open to receiving abundance and energy in all forms.

If you have knee, hip or joint issues, follow the instructions below as best you can, but do this pose in a way that feels comfortable for you. It's really not about the pose itself, it's about the breath and the intention you are holding.

✦ Bring your feet 3–4 feet apart depending upon your height (the taller you are, the wider the stance).

✦ Turn your feet out at 45 degrees so the heels are facing towards each other and bend your knees so your bottom sinks low.

✦ Engage (draw in) your belly to support your back, promote your posture and strengthen your core.

✦ Open your palms and raise your arms towards the sky.

Utkata Konasana: *Goddess pose*

✦ As you inhale, imagine that you are drawing the abundant and unlimited energy of the universe into your arms, and as you exhale, draw your arms down, palms towards your body, and bring the energy into your sacral centre (just between the navel and the pubic bone).

✦ Do this as many times as you need while holding the pose – I recommend 10.

✦ When you have finished, bring your hands into the prayer position, straighten your legs and heel toe them closer together.

✦ As you stand with your hands in prayer, take a few moments to breathe and honour yourself and your guides. If you feel drawn to any saints, angels, masters or guides, know that they are standing with you and honouring you.

✦ When you are ready, make a silent bow to yourself and the universe.

Here's your intention for the day:

*'Today I move into my flow.*

*I welcome the support of the universe.*

*I recharge my sacred senses and move with ease.*

*I know that my essence is divine, connected to all living things.*

*It feels so good to be held and supported in my flow.*

*And so it is.'*

### #ShareYourVibe
*'I am flowing freely, feeling held and supported by the light!'*

# IGNITE

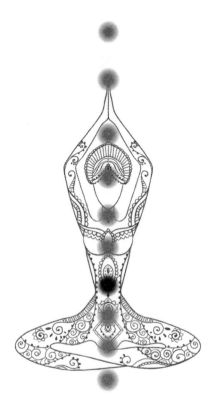

*Chakra:* Manipura (solar plexus)

*Location:* Just above the navel in the centre of the abdomen

*Colour:* Yellow

*Element:* Fire

*Manipura* is a Sanskrit word that means 'lustrous gem' and the solar plexus centre is the power centre of the whole body. On a clairvoyant level, it's perceived as a small circular sun that's spinning round and round. It governs our willpower and our ability to achieve in life. If it were in nature, it would be the sun that kisses the soil to give the warmth and tenderness needed for a seed to become a beautiful creation.

The part of the body related to this chakra is the digestive system. This chakra has everything to do with the tummy, how we process food and also how we process experiences in our life. It is the hub within us that ignites our intuition and what we know as our 'gut feelings'. Essentially it's the brain or central processing unit for all things 'feeling'. If you've ever had a feeling of nervousness at the beginning of a new job or a sense of sickness before something goes wrong in your life, that's the solar plexus activating.

In the next series of lessons you will ignite your willpower, focus your energy and fire up your sense of purpose. So get ready to blast through the blocks of doubt!

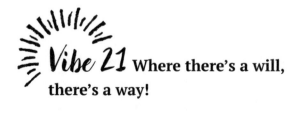

## *Vibe* 21 Where there's a will, there's a way!

Within you is a mighty power. You have the ability to achieve your dreams and create miracles in your life. Everything you do and everything you say is radiating out from you now and preparing the way forwards. You are a limitless being, suspended in a universe that is full, vibrant and unlimited in energy. It's with you now, it's in you now and it's got your back.

The power of intention is amazing – it's always working, even when you don't realize it. Everything that you say as a statement, sarcastic or not, is an intention. Every experience you accept into your life is also an intention. Now let me get this clear: I'm not telling you to stop having a joke and a laugh, but I am encouraging you to get clear about what you want to experience in the world.

Experiencing bad behaviour from others or feeling abused or taken advantage of can affect our intentions. To make it simple for you, it's like this. If a friend, colleague or partner starts to treat you in a way you don't feel is acceptable and you don't use your inner power to change it, the universe (even though it doesn't want this for you) will start to echo this type of experience in all four corners of your life *unless* you change it. It's as if magnetic waves from your thoughts and experiences move into your aura and attract similar energy, which then brings similar experiences into your life.

It's strangely easy to forget the fact that you are powerful and able to create amazing experiences, especially if life comes along and sweeps you up in a wave. A great tool that has helped me is being able to declare to the universe whether I feel something is in alignment with what I am ready to receive or not. For example, if something happens that I would like more of, I say: 'Yes, universe, this is what I'm talking about – this is exactly the sort of experience I enjoy and am open to receiving!'

I do exactly the same thing when something occurs that doesn't feel congruent with my path. I say: 'I'm grateful for this learning experience, but I am now choosing to clear from my aura all the thoughts, intentions and energy that have created this. I choose to have loving and supportive experiences in my life.'

# Vibe of the day

Today you are encouraged to cultivate the power of your will. Know that every one of your thoughts, feelings, actions and experiences is preparing the next experience of your life. If something doesn't feel right, clear it and restate your intention.

*'I am grateful that I can cultivate my life.*

*Every thought and feeling I have is creating my world.*

*I am ready to clear all thoughts and intentions that are not aligned with my happiness.*

*Today I choose to know that only good experiences lie before me.*

*My life is a joy and I choose to experience joy in all four corners of my life.*

*It feels so good to be in tune with the field of energy that moves through me.*

*I am safe.'*

# #ShareYourVibe
*'I choose to release challenge and embrace positive change.'*

# Vibe 22 Solar power, solar plexus

Our chakras are crucial to the raising of our vibration. I like to think of them as the spiritual anatomy, and when we look after that anatomy we are able to express more aspects of our true self and soul.

As we have seen, our solar plexus is important because it represents our willpower, our drive and our ability to achieve. It is the sun of our body. For this reason it's important to keep it balanced, energized and focused. When it's drained of energy, we can lose our drive and sense of direction and even be overwhelmed mentally. When it has too much energy moving through it, we can become addicted to being busy and have too many ideas we can't honour or follow through.

Maintaining a balanced solar plexus isn't as difficult as you might think. In fact it's so simple to be in touch with your solar plexus that it's easily forgotten by many on the spiritual path.

Your solar plexus allows you to access solar power from within so that you can create a sense of movement, excitement and ease in your life. As you maintain the balance of this space you allow your spiritual energy to move to a higher frequency and you are able to receive divine guidance and creative surges in a way that feels approachable and inspired.

# Vibe of the day

Today we will do a simple meditation exercise in which we encourage the solar plexus to move and radiate in a way that's balanced.

✦ Sit in a way that feels comfortable to you. Either on the floor or on a chair is completely cool.

✦ Encourage your shoulders to relax. Maybe roll them forwards and back a few times. Ease off your neck and roll it from side to side.

✦ Once you feel more comfortable, bring your hands to your solar plexus centre.

✦ Breathe into your hands. Feel your belly expand with each and every in-breath.

✦ Imagine that with every in-breath you are drawing light from the sun into your body and it's moving into the centre of your being. As this light comes into your body, it washes away all challenges, constrictions and conflicts from within. You move into a state of balance with your whole being.

✦ Stay there for as long as you need, breathing light into your solar plexus and exhaling the old and stale energy that has been standing between you and your inner power.

✦ When you're ready, set this intention:

> *'The sun of my soul is shining now.*
> *I am radiating with a harmonious light.*
> *I am in touch with divine inspiration.*
> *Creativity flows through me with ease.*
> *I am empowered and aligned with light.*
> *And so it is.'*

#### #ShareYourVibe
*'I have accessed the light of my soul and I share it with the world!'*

# Vibe 23 Your inner fire is to warm you, not burn you!

You are an inspired, spiritual and exciting individual. You have recognized that you have a larger part to play in this universe and you have responded to that call. You have learned that you have a solar light within you and you have recognized that you have divine inspiration moving through you at all times.

When you are receiving ideas and inspiration, it's important to know the universe always works on divine timing. It doesn't have any expectations of you, nor does it give you any time restrictions.

You are moving at the right pace for you and you are encouraged to acknowledge that. Your inner fire motivates you, encourages you and guides you.

The universe and its angels want to support you and your dreams. So take a step back and allow this divine support in. It's very easy to get sucked into a task or a dream, pour all of your energy into it and burn yourself out. Also, if you're always trying to be in control of a situation and can't take a step back to review where you are right now, there's a chance you're blocking your dream from happening. Your angels of light are with you now and they want you to know that it's important to stay interested in your goals, but don't put so much of your energy into them that you end up feeling drained and depleted. Draw on the support of the universe and trust in its divine timing.

## Vibe of the day

Today you are encouraged to take a step back and allow the universe to meet you halfway. Recognize that whatever dream or goal you are working on is coming to fruition in its own good time and that over-possessiveness can end up holding you back rather than taking you forwards.

Know that you have done what you need to and hand the rest over to the universe. Know angels are gladly taking over from here so you can be guided to your highest good.

✦ Imagine you are taking the situation that's worrying you or burning you out into your hands. Hold them wide open.

✦ Lift your hands up to heaven and imagine that an angel of golden light is taking this situation from you and taking it to heaven. Say:

> *'Today I hand this situation over to heaven.*
>
> *I am grateful for the support that is all around me.*
>
> *I trust that I am moving forwards in a way that is for my greater good.*
>
> *I allow the universe to meet me halfway.*
>
> *I am grateful for all of the steps I have taken and I honour them now.*
>
> *I have given my all and now I step back to receive.*
>
> *And so it is!'*

# #ShareYourVibe
*'I move into the balance of giving and receiving!'*

# Vibe 24 Say 'hello' to your ego!

Our ego has a radical plan of its own. It likes to throw a curve ball. It loves to tip us off-balance. When it likes, it can be one nasty piece of work. Most of us end up falling out with our ego, and when we do, we start a war in our own mind. It's time to change that.

The ego has a purpose. I know it's hard to think of it that way, but it's true. The ego is that voice within us that starts to write a plan for success and a plan for failure at the same time. It's the inner voice that makes us feel special and unworthy in the same sentence. It's the voice that gives us a *choice*.

The purpose of the ego is to give us the opportunity to be drawn in by fear or motivated by love. On some level, it's basically asking, 'Are you ready to move beyond your own limitations and fears?' The truth of the matter is that sometimes we're not.

When we're challenged by our ego and get sucked into the fear of failure and the war of unworthiness, there's a part of us that's saying, 'I need some more love in order to move up a step!' and we have to provide that love in order to be limitless rather than limited.

# Vibe of the day

Today you are encouraged to take a different approach to your ego. When this voice starts to babble, instead of telling it to shut up, you are encouraged to say 'hello' and send it some love.

As soon as you hear your inner voice making a false promise or telling you something that you know isn't your essential truth (which is that you are pure love), say:

'Hello, ego,

*Thanks for being there. Thanks for sharing your opinion and giving me the choice whether to listen or not.*

*Today I'm choosing to think differently, but thanks for popping by anyway.*

*Take care!'*

Then get on with your day.

Do it as many times you need to, using your own language. Say 'hello' and then let go.

#ShareYourVibe
*'Hello, ego, thanks for sharing.
I let go and let good in.'*

# Vibe 25 Sustain your self-worth!

How you see yourself and how you value yourself have everything to do with the raising of your vibration. When you begin to raise yourself up and get more connected, you begin to see yourself the way the universe and angels do.

Your self-worth is your true vision of yourself. It helps you recognize that you are deserving of growth and learning on this pathway. When you top it up, you move into a state of confidence with the ability to create success from a place that is loving and balanced.

It's so important to see yourself in a loving way. One of the greatest ways to do this is to look at yourself through the eyes of your guardian angel. Your guardian angel loves you unconditionally and has no expectations of you. They just fall in love with you each and every second. And they see beyond your looks and what we class as vanity – they see the light of your soul.

# Vibe of the day

Today you are encouraged to see yourself through the eyes of your guardian angel. Know that when they look at you they look beyond your health concerns, your financial status and the labels you have given yourself and see beautiful golden light. They see a being filled with potential in a space of unlimited possibility.

✦ Imagine yourself as golden light. See that you are unlimited on all levels.

✦ Know that you are loved beyond words. Today, choose to offer yourself that same love.

✦ Believe that your errors are behind you now and what you do with this moment is what matters.

✦ Say:

*'I am a being of unconditional love and light.*

*I am filled with unlimited potential.*

*I move beyond the errors and challenges of my past.*

*Today I choose to respect myself.*

*I choose to honour that I am a soul in a body.*

*I deserve to experience love in my life.*

*Today I offer myself this love.'*

### #ShareYourVibe
*'Today I choose to offer myself the love I deserve.'*

# ⚡ *Vibe 26* **Sleep right to shine bright!**

So many lightworkers switch on at night-time, not only on a mental level but on a spiritual level as well. A huge reason why we light up in the evening is that we don't have as many distractions around us then and we have the opportunity to hear our soul voice. But a good night's sleep is essential to raising your frequency.

In order to encourage a good night's sleep, you need to prepare yourself before you get into bed. Instead of jumping straight in and trying to sleep, especially if you know this is difficult, you can prepare your energy, set an intention and clear the space around you so that you can move with ease into deep and fulfilling rest.

Today's lesson is to be saved until it's time for bed – but check it out before then so you have time to prepare.

## *Vibe of the day*

To get a good night's sleep, here are the easiest three things you can do before you go to bed:

✦ *Clear the clutter.* Physical clutter is psychic clutter. If your sleeping space has too much stuff floating around in it, then your mind will too. Clear your space and you will feel clear within.

✦ *Meditate.* Sit on the floor next to your bed and meditate for 5–10 minutes. You don't have to go too deep, just do something to focus on your breathing. Do something that's blissful – maybe imagine walking along a beautiful beach. Let your mind wander if it needs to, but make your breathing as long and deep as possible. This will give you the time to let your mind wander instead of bringing that energy into bed with you.

✦ *Set an intention.* Once you've finished your meditation, set the intention to relax at bedtime. Speak clearly to the universe and tell it that this is not a time for you to work, get creative or rearrange your life. Be clear that you are ready to rest and that you are grateful for its support.

# #Share Your Vibe
*'When I sleep right, I shine bright!'*

# Vibe 27 Interact with your intuition

Your intuition is speaking to you every day. Every time you ask yourself a question, your intuition sends you an answer or impression to do with that situation. If you're like most of us, though, you don't listen to the subtle messages your intuition sends you and that's why you can never differentiate between guidance and fear.

Your intuition loves to support you and your growth. It is helped by a deep spiritual trait known as discernment. Discernment means knowing what's right for you – it's the ability to trust your inner promptings.

Although the universe speaks to you through your intuition, it honours your free will. So you are always free to ignore your intuition, even though this inner guidance system will be working for your highest good.

*A Course in Miracles* has a powerful quote that really speaks to my soul:

## 'The Holy Spirit's Voice is as loud as your willingness to listen.'

In this case the Holy Spirit's voice is your intuition. If you are willing to listen to it, you will learn to trust the feelings that come up as guidance and follow them.

As you follow the intuitive impulses you receive, you will raise your vibrations and your aura will be shining and golden.

# Vibe of the day

Today's lesson is a prompting to listen to the voice within. You are guided to hear what your soul has to share with you. Know that guidance from within will always be loving and will always speak in the present tense.

Spend time meditating with your soul today. Keep it simple.

✦ Close your eyes and visualize yourself immersed in golden light.

✦ Say:

> *'I am listening to my soul.'*

✦ Then ask:

> *'Where would you have me go today?'*
> *'What would you have me do today?'*

*'What would you have me say?'*
*'And to whom shall I say it?'*

✦ Listen to what your soul shares with you. Trust it. It will give you many home truths. Act on them and you will connect more strongly to your intuition.

#ShareYourVibe
*'I trust my vibes and respond to them accordingly.'*

## Vibe 28 Testament of trust

Trust is a big deal, especially these days. We've all had people lying to us and people lying about us. We've all also endured betrayal.

To raise your vibration successfully, it's important to surround yourself with people who are honest, trustworthy and loving. You need to be supported, you need to feel supported and you also need to be the supporting supporter – in order to encounter trustworthy people, you yourself need to be trustworthy.

Both friendships and relationships require a balance of giving and receiving. Sure, sometimes you have to give more and at other times you will be more in need, but true relationships will balance out and outshine the rest.

Being able to be honest in all relationships is crucial, because if you can't be, you're not being who you truly are. When you're holding back from saying something or are unable to share a deeper aspect of yourself because you fear (or know) you'll be made a mockery of or the information isn't safe with that person, it's time to change that.

I've found that if I want to have good friends in my life, I need to be a good friend too. If I want to have honesty, I have to be honest. If I want to feel honoured, I have to honour others.

# Vibe of the day

Today you are encouraged by the universe to offer support to those you love. Give thanks for the relationships you have in your world and ask yourself what you can do that's loving and supportive to those around you.

Being a good friend and sticking to your word go a long way. If you feel that you've not done this in the past, it's important to work on clearing that up now. Seek forgiveness where it is needed and offer support wherever you can in order to feel more supported in your world too.

To raise your vibration you need a level of trust in your life and so it's important to surround yourself with people you can trust and who can trust you.

Although today's task may not be done over 24 hours, it will enable you to feel more supported and balanced in your life.

#ShareYourVibe
*'I offer my support and trust to those I love.'*

# Vibe 29 Don't give shame all the fame

Feeling shame is more common than you think. Truth be told, we all feel some sort of shame now and then. There are always going to be things in our life we regret or that we wish we could change. There are also going to be various things about ourselves that we wouldn't like other people to know.

Shame is a hard, overwhelming and sometimes heavy emotion that is fuelled by the ego. It's a dark little memory that makes us feel inadequate, useless and stupid. But I believe challenging emotions are just another beautiful reminder that we're here to learn what love really is.

One way to move beyond shame is to recognize something that's true. It might sound super bumper sticker, but here's something that's helped me countless times. When I feel shame, I tell myself this:

### 'Without the darkness, the stars could not shine!'

When the darkness of shame arrives, it's giving you the opportunity to be a star and shine.

## Vibe of the day

Today's lesson looks easy but it will challenge you. In order to stop giving shame all the fame you have to drop something else: comparison.

Shame makes you feel low because your ego tries to compare your experience to someone else's experience or to what it thinks is perfect. Either way, you are led down the road to not feeling good enough.

Today you are being invited by the universe to stop comparing yourself (and others) to the way you think things should be. Trust that everyone is doing their best with the knowledge they have – and that includes you. You have no need to feel shame because you've always done your best. Know this. Offer this gift to everyone you know.

#ShareYourVibe
'Shame can only exist when I compare myself to others. I release the need to compare.'

## Vibe 30 Ignite your light!

Your solar energy is strong now. You are balanced. Free of shame. Filled with inspiration. In touch with your inner voice and integrated with your intuition.

You were made to shine. Your light is within you now and the world is ready to see it.

Today you are invited to turn your light on in a conscious way and to send it out into the world. You are invited to do this whole process with a simple pose.

# *Vibe of the day*

+ Bring your feet together. Separate your heels slightly if this is uncomfortable.

+ Squeeze your inner thighs towards each other and gently scoop your bottom underneath you.

+ Draw your belly in lightly to generate energy in your solar plexus centre.

+ Roll your shoulders back and have your palms at your sides facing forwards. Welcome to *Tadasana* or 'Mountain pose'.

Tadasana: *Mountain pose*

+ Imagine that you are turning a light on in your belly. This light is shining more and more brightly until it is shining all the way through your body. The drawing-in of your belly is encouraging this light to move up and down your spine and through all the major extremities of your body.

✦ That light moves to your hands. As you feel it reach them, sweep them up into the air.

✦ Drawing your shoulders down (which keeps the chest engaged and the heart open), imagine that you are sending that light of yours to the four corners of the world. You aren't losing your energy but sharing it with the entire world.

✦ Once you feel you have done this you can bring your hands back down to your heart centre in prayer style and make a silent bow to yourself.

✦ Celebrate the fact that you've finally embraced your light and shared it with the world!

### #ShareYourVibe
*'Today I ignite my light and shine brightly in the world!'*

# RECEIVE

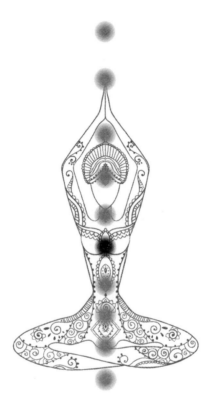

*Chakra:* Anahata (heart)

*Location:* The centre of the chest/heart region

*Colour:* Green (sometimes turns pink or ruby)

*Element:* Air

*Anahata* is a Sanskrit word that means 'unstruck' and it brings us the beautiful idea that our heart can never really be broken. This chakra is linked to our ability to give and receive love. In order to live a spiritually awakened life we have to find a balance between giving and receiving in order to allow the higher heart (the next part of the heart chakra) to awaken. If the heart chakra were in nature it would be the blissful wind that carries the pollen through the air and the insects that pollinate plants and encourage them to grow.

The parts of the body related to this chakra are the heart, lungs and upper respiratory system. It governs all issues of the heart, including experiencing love, relationships and even break-ups. Although we feel heartbreak when we lose someone we love or face the end of a relationship, the Anahata chakra helps us move beyond ideas of separation and limitation and realize that the soul (the spiritual heart) can never be tarnished or broken. This idea helps us heal.

The lessons that follow will help you move beyond the ideas of limitation and loss into a space that is fulfilled and whole. You are guided to work your heart chakra and open it in order to receive the blessings you deserve in your life.

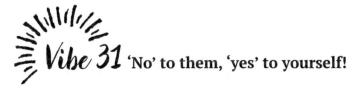

# *Vibe 31* 'No' to them, 'yes' to yourself!

The universe knows that a lot of this raising your vibes stuff is to do with how you want to help the world, and probably those around you too. When you want to give, it shows that you have a wonderfully generous, kind and loving heart – it shows you want to make a difference. But let's talk about receiving for a change.

When you receive, you allow yourself to be replenished with all that you have given and more. And you deserve to be replenished, because you share so much with the world. Know this.

It's never easy to strike a balance between giving and receiving, but your soul will tell you when you need to receive rather than give. If someone is asking you for a favour and you're really unable to oblige but do so anyway because you feel guilty or that if you don't do it you're letting someone down, you should know that you're letting yourself down if you give in.

Today's lesson is a gentle kick in the butt from the universe because it wants you to be replenished. It wants you to have the tools to say 'no' to others so you can finally say 'yes' to yourself. This is self-care 101.

# Vibe of the day

Today you are encouraged to say 'yes' to yourself. How can you do this? What can you do to feel replenished? Is there anything on your agenda that you can gently let go? Is there something you can do for yourself?

If you are under pressure from others, here's a tool for saying 'no' in a loving way so you can look after yourself:

*'I am sorry you feel like that/that you are overwhelmed and I want nothing but the best for you. You deserve to be happy. But right now I can't help you with that. So I'm going to say "no" to you so that I can say "yes" to myself. Thank you for understanding. I love you.'*

You can say this in conversation or you can just say it quietly to yourself. If it's someone you don't love, you can adjust it accordingly, but you get the idea.

*'Today I say "yes" to myself.*
*I replenish all of my needs.*
*Today I say "yes" to myself.*
*I set myself free!'*

# *Vibe 32* Make way for miracles

Are miracles happening in your life? I believe we are all entitled to them.

A miracle is a shift in perception – it's changing the way you think. It can be as simple as choosing a loving thought over one that's filled with fear.

According to *A Course in Miracles*, no miracle is greater or smaller than another, because a change of thinking creates them all. As you know, I like to take it a little bit further and recognize that it's not about how big a miracle is but about how much room you create in your life for it.

Miracles occur as natural expressions of love. When they don't occur, something has gone wrong. You could be thinking positively and trying to stay focused on love, but at the same time not be able to understand how things could change.

You can't allow your mind to get in the way of your ability to manifest beautiful miracles in your life – you just have to create the space for them and let the angels do the rest.

# Vibe of the day

Today you are encouraged to make space for the miracles you deserve in your life. If there's a situation you know needs a miracle, you have to take the first steps and then let the universe meet you halfway.

Instead of trying to do the maths and work out what has to happen next or how something could possibly change, feed the situation with love and then hand it over to the universe and the angels of light that dance through the cosmos.

Your job is not to perform miracles, just to create the space for them to happen. Send love to the areas of your life that need a miracle today and imagine them being held in the hand of your creator.

See your angels dancing and supporting you as you accept the miracles you deserve.

*'Today I make space for miracles.*

*I recognize that it's not how big a miracle is that's important but how much room I create for it.*

*I send love to all the situations in which I need support.*

*I allow myself to feel supported.*

*Miracles occur naturally and I welcome them with an open heart.'*

#ShareYourVibe
*'I make way for miracles!'*

# *Vibe 33* Miraculous masters

The ascended masters are a congregation of enlightened souls, divine beings and angels who are dedicated to the peace and nurturing of the planet. These amazing masters go beyond religion and transcend time, and they are willing to help all who call on them. I like to call them 'the keepers of light'.

The reason I am mentioning the masters at this time is because 33 is a number closely associated with one of the greatest ascended masters of our time: Jesus. It is believed that he lived to the tender age of 33, and when this number comes up constantly in your life, the keepers of light are offering their assistance to you.

There are many masters that you can call upon and you will connect with many of them as you progress through this book. Most are great sages or teachers who once walked this Earth like you and me – people like Joan of Arc, Paramahansa Yogananda, Master Buddha and Kuan Yin, to name but a few. They went on deep spiritual journeys and when their body died, they chose to continue their mission from the other side.

There is a great chance that you are already drawn to a saint, teacher, master or spiritual guide in heaven. You are encouraged to know that they are with you now, helping you walk this path.

# Vibe of the day

You are encouraged to call upon the ascended masters, spiritual guides and enlightened teachers you are drawn to. Allow yourself to have a free-flowing conversation with them. Thank them for being close, for guiding you along your path and for helping you understand the lessons that are occurring in your life today.

Reinstate what you already know: that you do not walk this path alone and you are supported by a presence of light who can guide you. Make space for that presence with the following words:

*'I welcome and accept the help of transcended teachers.*

*I am grateful to know that ascended masters are guiding my path.*

*It feels so good to walk this path feeling supported.*

*Thank you, spiritual guides, for helping me understand where I am.*

*Thank you, divine masters, for helping me embrace my gifts and lessons.*

*And so it is!'*

## #ShareYourVibe
*'I acknowledge the spiritual guides who support me on my path!'*

# Vibe 34 Welcome to the cave of your heart

As I mentioned earlier, the heart chakra is known as *Anahata* in Sanskrit, which means 'unstruck' and reminds us of an extremely important lesson: the heart can never be broken.

This lesson may challenge you slightly, because we've all experienced being broken-hearted for a number of different reasons, but mainly losing someone who's important to us or having a relationship end.

The universe wants you to know that your heart can never be broken, but your ego can convince you otherwise. The feeling of heartbreak is created when we feel separated from someone we love. Although this will feel very real, it is an illusion, because it contradicts everything we know to be true on a soul level.

On a soul level we know that we are love and that love moves through the entire universe, uniting us as one. We are one. We are connected to everyone and everything that is, was and ever will be through the cave of our heart, but for some reason the world convinces us that we can be separate.

It's time to regroup those feelings and move back into the wave of love that sent you here – it's time to ride that wave.

## Vibe of the day

+ Place your hands on your heart and breathe deeply into them.

+ Realize that there are two hearts within you: the heart that is an organ and the heart that represents your capacity to know and experience love.

✦ Then set this intention:

*'Today I acknowledge the wholeness of my heart.*
*I realize that this true part of me will never be broken.*
*I am divine, unstruck and well.'*

#ShareYourVibe
*'The heart of my soul is always healed and whole.'*

# Vibe 35 Love is not lost

When it comes to love, if we're not experiencing it in our life, we tend to go looking for it. We search for it in things, people and even experiences, but when we're looking for it, we'll never find it.

*A Course in Miracles* has an approach to love that is simple in words, but will challenge you in action:

**'Your task is not to seek for love, but merely to seek and find all the barriers within yourself that you have built against it.'**

Love is ever-present. It's the essence that creates the very being that you are. When all fear is stripped down, it's only love that's left. Within the depths of your being is a love that is unconditional, and it's waiting for you to arrive. The outer world convinces you that you are separate from love, but the inner world says different.

# Vibe of the day

All your grudges, fears and frustrations are barriers that stand in the way of love. Every time you think about any of these things you are spending less time on experiencing the higher love that you deserve. Today you are encouraged to seek and remove all your barriers to love.

Right now you will be made aware of people and situations you need to make peace with in order to move on.

✦ Who do you need to forgive?

✦ What isn't serving you? Can you let it go?

✦ Where in your life can you drop the need to be right in order to be happy?

Here is a prayer:

> *'Thank you, universe, for helping me see the barriers within myself that are standing in the way of love. I am ready and willing to remove these barriers so I can move into the deeper and truer aspects of myself. I surrender.*
>
> *And so it is!'*

## #ShareYourVibe
*'Love is always present. Today I welcome that gift.'*

# *Vibe 36* Give generously, receive graciously

The universe is all about balance. You've heard about it already. People call it 'karma' or 'the law of cause and effect'. We've mentioned already that karma is the law that encourages us to be kind. And as we give out kindness, it comes back and kisses us.

Giving and receiving work like this too. As you give, you are making room in your life to receive. When you give to others graciously and without expectation, the universe needs to give to you. It's so simple, but we find it hard to accept.

The path of a lightworker is a generous path. You give without needing to receive because that's who you are. You are a light and it's in your nature to give, but today you are being encouraged to receive.

The heart chakra is the space within you that represents kindness and altruism. It's the part of you that wants to share with those you feel are in need. When you give graciously, your heart chakra opens up and shines brightly.

You know how good it is to give someone a gift (no matter the size) that you've put a lot of thought into and to see them enjoy it. You know how good it is to help someone out, even if it's just offering a hand to someone at the train station struggling to get their luggage down the steps. It feels good to give.

But your heart chakra can become drained when you give too much. When this happens, you'll get frustrated at yourself and feel that you can't give any more. In order to maintain a sense of balance in your life, it is your spiritual duty to receive.

# Vibe of the day

Today you are encouraged to let the universe know that you are willing to receive. You are encouraged to welcome offers of help, support and kindness into your life. If someone at work offers you a hand, accept it. If someone offers to cook you dinner or lunch, welcome it! More importantly, if someone gives you a compliment, receive it and honour yourself.

Smile. Breathe. Receive.

*'I am willing to receive.*

*I have recognized that I am deserving of help, love and support.*

*It feels good to give and it feels great to receive.*

*Today I welcome the energy of balance into my life.*

*My heart is open to receive.'*

#ShareYourVibe
*'I am ready to receive!'*

# Vibe 37 Loving yourself enough

Loving yourself is probably one of the more challenging aspects of raising your vibration. The reason that this can be hard is because the ego likes to challenge you on it. Every time you move into a more loving space, the ego will create its own plan or tell you what you don't want to hear.

The ego, as we learned a few lessons ago, is just doing its job. It's giving you the opportunity to trust what you know to be true.

It's important to say here that the ego is going to tell you stuff that you've already heard. Everything that you hear on a negative level is something you've already told yourself in the past, something you've sabotaged yourself with. Now it's time for it to go.

Loving yourself enough means truly honouring who you are. It's that moment when you decide you're no longer going to be represented by negative opinion, fear or anything else that's come between you and your goodness in the past.

Loving yourself doesn't always mean looking in the mirror and telling yourself, 'I love you!' It can also be about the decisions you make in your life. Here are some examples of self-love:

✦ Moving into a state of forgiveness with others because it removes the toxicity from within you.

✦ Not allowing others to treat you badly.

✦ Giving yourself time to do the things you love.

# Vibe of the day

Today you are encouraged to love yourself enough. Enough in the sense of doing something for yourself or saying something to yourself that you would normally hold back on.

In your act of self-love, realize that you are able to draw more universal light into yourself and raise your vibration to its optimum strength. Your ability to love yourself and respect who you are will become a healing wave that inspires those around you.

*'Today I choose to love myself enough to say "no"
to bad behaviour or toxic emotions and make
room in myself to be nourished by light.*

*I realize that how I see myself has everything
to do with how the world sees me.*

*I choose to look at myself in a loving way and allow that
loving wave to wash from me and throughout the world.*

*Today I love myself enough to make the changes
I need to feel loved and accepted.'*

#ShareYourVibe

*'Loving yourself enough is saying "no" to toxic
emotions and "yes" to forgiveness.'*

# *Vibe 38* Forgive doesn't mean forget

There's an old saying that I've heard too many times: 'I'll forgive, but I'll never forget,' and quite honestly it makes me shudder.

Forgiveness is a complex process. It definitely isn't the easiest subject to explain either. So many interpretations go along with it – it means something different for everyone. For me, forgiveness means remembering that you can never really be hurt, because nothing can tarnish your soul. It's the moment when you choose no longer to be defined by the sadness or the hurt of a situation. It doesn't mean forgetting, but choosing something that's working for you.

Forgiveness is choosing loving thoughts instead of difficult memories or what I call 'nightmares' that tie you to a situation in the past. It isn't about letting someone off or accepting their bad behaviour, it's just choosing to focus on the positive instead.

## Vibe of the day

Today you take your power back and decide to focus on memories and emotions that are working in your favour. Instead of choosing a memory or a feeling that drags you down, now is the time to reprogram your brain and energy with something that feels safe and loving.

Your ego will try to fight. Don't fight. Just decide to focus on something else. Tell your ego you're focusing on something else.

When a painful memory comes up, go to a thought that's loving. Here are some suggestions:

✦ Think about someone you love.

✦ Imagine your guardian angel is swooping you up in their wings of love.

✦ Think of your favourite flower. Imagine its sweet scent.

✦ Remind yourself that only love is real.

### #ShareYourVibe
'Forgiving doesn't mean forgetting, it means choosing to remember love instead.'

# *Vibe 39* Open hands, open heart!

Our hands are an extension of our heart. Our heart sends its energy through our arms and we express that love with our hands. In energy healing, including Reiki, the hands become the instrument of light when it comes to sharing the healing.

In our daily life we use our hands to describe how we feel. When we see someone we love or are spending time with them, we may hold their hand. As we do so, we are filled with a deep sense of connection and love, and it's because we are literally sharing each other's energy from the heart through the hands.

We unconsciously use our hands in many ways. You've probably crossed your arms to protect your heart and squeezed your hands together when you've been nervous. You clap to express joy and wave to share goodwill. Your hands are a powerful expression of who you are.

When you meditate, your palms can do different things. I've always gone with the idea that open palms means an open heart and it's always helped me.

## Vibe of the day

Today you are encouraged to see how your hands express who you are. How do you connect with others, how do you share your feelings and how open is your heart with your hands?

✦ Take a moment to meditate today, either sitting on a chair, on the floor, in the car or wherever you happen to be.

✦ Open your palms and rest them on your knees.

✦ Allow your palms to draw in fresh energy and allow it to flow to your heart.

#ShareYourVibe
*'I open my hands and my heart!'*

# Vibe 40 Believe to receive

We're always convinced that we're separate from everything else, but we're not. All of the world's great spiritual teachers will tell you that you are one with everything. That's what's happening when you see your spiritual signs like 11:11: you are being reminded that what you seek is a part of you now.

People used to say to me, especially when I was starting out, 'I'll believe it when I see it!' but they've got it all wrong. The truth of the matter is, you will receive what you seek when you believe you have it already.

In the *Bhagavad Gita*, India's leading spiritual text, Krishna, the main spiritual guide/representative of God, tells Arjuna, the leading character:

> *'When a person is devoted to something*
> *with complete faith, I unify his faith in that.*
> *Then when his faith is completely unified,*
> *he gains the object of his devotion.'*

What are you searching for? What do you seek? You have the answers, the connection and the abundance within you now. Believe it.

# Vibe of the day

Today you are encouraged to see that you have the universe within you now. Every strand and cell of your body and being is in touch with everything that is, was and ever will be.

All that you seek is within you now. Go within and draw it to you now. Say:

*'My life is a manifestation of my thoughts and feelings.*

*I am capable of manifesting miracles.*

*I am ready to believe and receive.*

*And so it is!'*

### #ShareYourVibe
*'I believe and then receive!'*

# EXPRESS

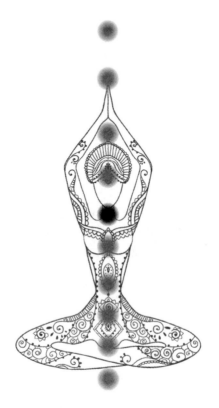

*Chakra:* Vishuddha (throat)
*Location:* The neck, throat and thyroid gland
*Colour:* Blue
*Element:* Space

*Vishuddha* is a Sanskrit word that means 'purification'. It is the name of the spiritual energy centre that governs our ability to speak our truth and express our emotional self. If the throat chakra were in nature it would be the song of nature – the songs of the birds and the howls of the wolves and the roars of the lions.

What we experience on this Earth has a lot to do with what frequency we give off, what we say and what we don't, and the throat chakra allows us to access our truth in order to experience a life that is filled with integrity.

It also relates to our emotional self – how we express our emotions, how much we hold in and how honest we are both with others and ourselves.

Within the body, the Vishuddha chakra looks after the throat, neck and thyroid gland and can also have a lot to do with the ears, as they are critical to the ability to hear and be heard.

The lessons that you are about to delve into will help you to express yourself through your voice and your emotions and encourage you to be deeply honest with yourself. As you move into the energy of true self-expression, you raise your vibration high and stand honest and pure with the universe.

# *Vibe 41* Neck check!

So we've been working our way through the chakras, the energy centres of the body, to help raise our vibration. The next one up is the throat chakra. This chakra represents our ability to communicate, create and purify our body with ease. It governs the neck, throat and ears. In order for its energy to be clearly expressed, it's important to look after these areas of the body.

From a personal point of view, I've found the neck goes through a lot. I practise yoga frequently and have had to become more conscious of when I'm straining my neck in postures, especially if there's a particular gazing point. I've found that having a more relaxed neck and being more fluid with the neck have left me feeling clearer about my creativity and ability to express myself.

The throat chakra is the physical space where the weight of the world can sit right on the top of our shoulders, and if it's out of alignment, our neck feels as though it's crooked. It's time for you to relax the area physically and clear the space energetically to make room for yourself and your truth.

# Vibe of the day

Today you are encouraged to relax, stretch and care for your neck.

✦ Sitting either on a chair or in a simple cross-legged position on the floor, bring both of your hands to your knees, with the palms face down for grip and support.

✦ Inhale and squeeze your shoulders up to your ears.

✦ Exhale and roll your shoulders down and away from your head.

✦ Take several deep breaths and allow your neck to relax.

✦ Moving with your breath, inhale through your nose as you gaze upwards, then exhale through your mouth (creating a 'haaaa' noise like a wave) and begin to tuck your chin under you. (You are essentially slowly nodding your head.)

✦ Do this about 8–10 times.

✦ Now inhale through your nose as you look left.

✦ Exhale through your mouth as you look straight ahead.

+ Inhale through your nose as you look right.

+ Exhale through your mouth as you look straight ahead.

+ Do this about 8–10 times.

+ Relax. Receive.

> *'Today I take the weight of the world*
> *off my neck and shoulders.*
>
> *I make the energetic space to express who I truly am.'*

*#ShareYourVibe*
*'I create space within my life to*
*express my true self.'*

# *Vibe 42* Express your emotions and experiences

Expressing your emotions is never the easiest thing to do, but it's important. We all know what it's like to hold back when it comes to something emotional. Think about the term 'lump in your throat' – you know what that is, right? If there's a physical lump in your throat because of an emotional situation, what's happening on an energetic level?

If we don't express the energy or emotions that come with an experience and just hold them all in, the energy of our throat chakra – the expressive centre of our body – becomes clogged up and so do we.

When the throat chakra is clogged up, a range of different things can happen in our life that feel like a roadblock. Here are some examples:

✦ losing our voice

✦ having problems with our teeth, throat or gums

✦ bad breath

✦ thyroid challenges

✦ constantly feeling dry in the mouth

✦ speaking but not being heard

✦ speaking but being misinterpreted

Are any of these familiar? If so, today's lesson is extremely important for you because there is stale energy building up that's ready to be released.

# Vibe of the day

Today you are encouraged to express your feelings and experiences with grace. If there's something you've been holding back from saying, now is the time to free yourself. When you share your feelings, you create space within yourself for miracles to enter. When you free yourself of a feeling, you give yourself love. When you express your feelings, you perform an act of self-love. When you honour your feelings, you hold the space to be honoured.

If you are unsure of how to say something to the world, just say it to yourself first. Have an honest conversation with yourself – let out how you truly feel. Once you have reached that deep state of honesty, hand over the reins to the universe and allow it to lead the way.

> *'Thank you, universe, for surrounding me with support
> and light. I hand this situation entirely over to you.
> Thank you for directing me in ways that I can recognize
> so that I can express my true feelings. It feels good
> to be honest with you, myself and those I love. I am
> ready to express my emotions and experiences.'*

### #ShareYourVibe

*'Expressing your emotions and
experiences is an act of self-love.'*

## Vibe 43 The breath of life

Breathing is so important. In ancient yogic texts we are taught that the breath represents *prana*, which is the Sanskrit word for 'life-force'. So, when we are breathing deeply we are drawing divine light energy into our body.

Breathing is instinctive: we do it without thinking from the first few moments after we are born. When I lead a yoga class I always encourage people to remember this. If they forget about their breath or hold it in, they are letting a basic instinct drop.

Most people breathe quickly when they are late. They hold their breath if they are under pressure or facing a challenge. But these are the moments when we need life-force the most – these are the moments when we are encouraged to breathe.

Quite simply, your breath regenerates your body. It brings oxygen to your cells. It keeps you alive.

Our lung capacity is actually quite large, but we generally don't use all of it. Most people who are under pressure only breathe using the top part of the lungs, which means that the top of the chest and the throat area are receiving a great deal of the energy but it's not extending much further than that.

When too much energy builds up in one place like this, we add to our stress rather than relieve it. And if energy is already building up in the throat area and then we bring life-force in through our breath and that builds up there too, things start to get a bit crowded.

# Vibe of the day

Today you are encouraged to breathe using the full capacity of your lungs. As you do this, you draw pure white life-force into the whole of your being, rejuvenating your physical body and spiritual anatomy.

Let this simple breathing technique be something you come back to time and time again:

✦ Bring your hands to your abdomen. Place one hand on each side of your belly and breathe into them. Feel the natural rhythm of your breath flowing in and out of your body. Do this for 8–10 breaths.

✦ Bring your hands to your sides. Wrap them around your ribcage and breathe into them. Feel your diaphragm expand with each and every in-breath. Do this for 8–10 breaths.

✦ Place your fingers on your collarbone. Allow your hands to rest gently on your chest and breathe into your hands. Feel your chest lift and your throat fill with *prana* with each and every breath. Do this for 8–10 breaths.

✦ When you have finished this sequence of breaths, you may want to do it without your hands, simply by breathing into all these spaces. Linking the breath in the belly, middle body and upper body forms the full yogic breath, which connects body, mind and soul.

### #ShareYourVibe
*'When I forget to breathe, I forget my instincts. Today I choose to remember my breath and breathe with ease. Breathing is instinctive.'*

## Vibe 44 Hello, angels!

You have a guardian angel who has been with you from the moment you chose to come to Earth. This being of pure white light will be with you until you return to the heart of the universe.

Angels are the heartbeats of the universe. As far as I'm concerned, they are extensions of universal love coming to us in personal form. Our relationship with our guardian angel reflects our relationship with the universal life-force.

Angels don't want to be worshipped and they don't want us to bow down to them, they just want us to experience happiness and peace on Earth.

Since I met my guardian angel well over 12 years ago I haven't gone a day without speaking to him or sending a prayer to the angels in general. Angels respond to our prayers and our thoughts. I have learned that they *love* to be thanked – not because they enjoy the praise or the feeling of being powerful but because when we thank them our perception is moving from lack to plenty.

# Vibe of the day

Today you are encouraged to hang out with your guardian angel. Your angel loves you unconditionally and honours your free will and will never override it unless it is a life-or-death situation. So the only way you'll be able to experience your angel is by accepting that they are close to you and inviting them into your life.

Know that every second your angel falls deeper and deeper in love with the light that you are. One day you will see your own light for yourself.

Today you are encouraged to look out for reminders that your angel is close by. You may find a feather, see the number 44 (the angels' number) jumping out at you or even hear a song on the radio with a message from them.

Work with the following prayer today and whenever you feel drawn to experience the presence of your guardian angel:

'Hello, guardian angel!

*It's so good to know you are here with me now and looking after me and my life. I am so grateful to know that I don't walk this path without you and that I have your support. Today I open myself up to you, your presence and your help.*

*Thank you for reminding me of your presence,
for revealing to me what I need to know and
for sending me signs that you are there.*

*Thank you, thank you, thank you!*

*And so it is!'*

#ShareYourVibe
*'I love to hang out with the angels!'*

# Vibe 45 Intuitive integrity

You are far more intuitive than you realize. The truth is you are receiving guidance every minute of the day. But sometimes you may find it difficult to discern if what you are hearing is based on fear or love.

When you hear a voice speak within you, especially when you are meditating or praying, you will probably wonder if what you are hearing is your imagination or your ego pushing the self-destruct button. It's time for you to know intuitively what is right for you.

Within you is a soul, and that soul has a voice. This voice is your inner guide, your inner teacher and a force that wants nothing but the best for you.

The ego always has a plan. It will always speak in the past or future tense. If you hear a voice telling you to do something and in so many days, weeks or months you'll see the results, this is the ego speaking. If you hear a voice telling you that if you don't make a certain change or do a particular thing you'll have bad luck, you'll fail, you'll get fat and ugly and you'll be a reject, then this is the ego too.

The voice of your soul will always speak in the present tense. It will speak to you in a loving way and it will always point out how far you've come, the gifts that you have and tell you that you have more strength than you know. The voice of your soul doesn't always have a plan but will remind you that if you take a step forwards the universe will present the next step to you. It encourages you to take a leap of faith, knowing that you will be caught by your angels and guides.

## Vibe of the day

Today, have a loving conversation with your soul voice to encourage it to speak to you loud and clear. Ask your angel guides to help you tap in to the guidance of your inner teacher so that you can follow your true heart's desire and take steps towards living your life filled with grace and purpose.

*'Thank you, soul, for being such a great teacher. I am overwhelmed with joy to know that you have been speaking to me and I promise that I have done everything I could to follow your guidance.*

*Thank you, angels, for helping me intuitively discern the voice of my soul so I can move towards a life that is filled with integrity and purpose.*

*I realize that the voice of my soul is loud when I am ready to listen.*

*Today I am ready to hear, so let me hear loud and clear.*

*And so it is!'*

#ShareYourVibe
'Today I choose to listen to the voice of my soul!'

## Vibe 46 My truth is my teacher

It's not always easy to say what you want to say, especially if you're worried you're going to upset someone or let them down. Speaking your truth, either by doing something you know you need to do, revealing information to set yourself free or telling someone how you really feel, is a huge spiritual lesson. It's the moment you step into your power and allow your spiritual energy to expand.

When you don't follow your truth, you put massive roadblocks in your path.

Truth is a great teacher because it allows you to move into a place of deep spiritual integrity where you honour and love yourself enough to admit what you really need to admit.

If you know you are at a point where you have something to say to another person or to your company or whatever, it's time to make some space in your life by speaking your truth.

If you're worried about what's going to happen next then you must know that the universe always has a better plan for you. And in order to take the next step you must take the first one. No one said this path was easy, right? But this is the lifetime in which you chose to up your spiritual connection and raise your vibration and to do that you have to be honest with yourself and everyone around you.

# *Vibe of the day*

In order to speak your truth to the world with clarity, integrity and grace, it's important to have a loving conversation with yourself. Tell yourself that everything's going to be totally cool and that you have more than enough support around you to make this decision. Remind yourself to speak your truth in a loving way. This honours the other person too by giving them the truth about a situation.

Tell yourself that you are more than good enough. Tell yourself that you are divine light and that you've made all your past decisions based on the information, awareness and intelligence you had at the time. You know that's true. Tell yourself that when you open up on an honest level, you will be liberated.

*Now speak your truth in a loving way.*

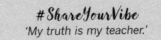

### #ShareYourVibe
'My truth is my teacher.'

# *Vibe 47* Commune and communicate

Hopefully by this point in your 111 spiritual techniques you're feeling clear about your communication abilities. The more clearly we communicate on Earth with our friends, lovers and families, the more clearly we are able to commune with the divine.

Having a loving, open and insightful conversation with the divine is so important. When we really open up about our feelings, thoughts, worries and decisions, we give that divine presence the space to enter our life and support us.

Our angels, our guides and the universal life-force itself are always with us – they are here right now – but in order for them to support us we have to give them the space and permission to support us. They do know a lot of our thoughts and feelings, but they can't always interact with them because they are ours, they are private, and the universe will not go against our free will.

When you open up and set the intention that you are clearly communicating with the presence of love that is part of who you are and with all of the heavenly support that surrounds you, your conversation will ride a wave of prayer to the heart of the divine. The divine always hears these conversations and, like an echo of deep love, a wave of healing, help and support will come back to you.

# Vibe of the day

It's time to have a loving conversation with the divine. It doesn't matter how you see the divine – it could be in the form of a particular saint, ascended master, angel, deity or even the cosmos – but know that it is ready and willing to listen.

The universe is always more willing to help you than you are to be helped. It's time to open up and recognize that the divine is your greatest love, your best ally and your truest friend. Speak to it in a way that's open. Share your concerns, reveal your feelings, let out your emotions and breathe with ease.

'Universe,

I am grateful for your love and support. Thank
you for hearing me clearly at this time and
for washing waves of love and light over
the areas of my life where I have concerns.
I know you are my greatest friend, ally and
love. I accept your love and support now.

Thank you, thank you, thank you!'

*#ShareYourVibe*
'The universe is my greatest ally, love and support.'

# *Vibe 48* Vibrational sounds

Sound is a powerful tool. Music especially is a medium of miracles
that allows us to access deeper aspects of ourselves. When I
learned that the human heartbeat mirrored the tempo of music, I
wasn't surprised. For me, music is the language of love.

When you listen to music that speaks to your soul, I believe you
raise your vibration really high. When you dance to music you
love or when you listen deeply, meditate or relax to music that
touches you, not only does your heart reflect the beat but your
spiritual heart opens to receive higher-vibrational energy, healing
and insight.

There's a powerful track that I often use at my spiritual seminars
to crack everyone open. It's a track that I've seen bring huge shifts
of love and healing and it allows people to feel completely open to

the divine. It is 'A Hundred Thousand Angels' by Lucinda Drayton. Whenever I play this, something within me just opens up.

I remember hearing Lucinda sing it live at the Mind Body Spirit Festival on 11/11/11 at 11:11 a.m. and my heart just about burst open. There I am, standing on a podium with a few thousand people in front of me, supposed to be holding space for light to enter, and as Lucinda is singing her song with deep grace and integrity, I am an emotional wreck.

Okay, I wasn't really a wreck. It was more that I was holding space within me for universal love to enter. I was allowing divine love to be with me on a full body level and ever since then I've made space in my life to do that with music.

# Vibe of the day

Today you are encouraged to look out that track that makes your heart feel as if it's about to explode. Which song makes you feel open, naked and connected to a presence of love that goes beyond your human comprehension? Look it out, play it on your laptop, phone, CD player or whatever other fancy gadget you have, and let it sing you into the presence of love that resides deep within you.

If you feel tears leaving your body, allow them to go as a light-filled life-force pervades your entire being. Breathe and know you are connected to something greater.

### #ShareYourVibe
*'Music allows my heart to open up and celebrate the love that's everlasting.'*

# Vibe 49 Om your way home!

According to many Eastern belief systems, in the beginning there was 'Om', the universal sound of creation. It wasn't just a sound – it was a vibration moving through the whole universe, the seed of the ultimate life-force.

It is for this reason that yoga, meditation and mindfulness classes alike chant 'Om', maybe following a tradition or spiritual lineage but also as a spiritual tool to connect them to something greater.

Whenever I chant 'Om' it's as if a vibration of peace moves through the very core of my being. I feel that I am singing the song of creation and I am honouring all of the great ancient sages and spiritual teachers who have gone before me.

'Om' is also used at the beginning and end of all the sacred spiritual teachings of the East, including the Vedas and the Upanishads, two of India's most influential collections of spiritual texts.

I really became interested in chanting a few years ago and after visiting India several times to practise yoga and meditation, I have really come to honour and resonate with the sound of 'Om'.

When we 'Om', on some level we acknowledge that we are part of the greater picture of life.

# Vibe of the day

Today it's time to chant 'Om'.

When you chant 'Om', you move into the universal vibration that flows through you and connects you to everything, everyone and every space that is, was and ever will be.

When you chant 'Om', your chakras spin and open up your divine connections and your personal vibration is lifted to the divine.

When you chant 'Om', you are taken back to heaven and you create heaven on Earth.

Take a deep breath and chant: 'Om...'

Hold it for as long as you can and feel that sense of connection with all that is and all that ever will be.

To make it easy to get into that sound, why not practise your 'Oms' in the car or wherever else you are on your own? I 'Om' on the way to yoga and to work and on the way home, just to move my physical self into that vibration of oneness.

#ShareYourVibe
*'"Om" is the vibration of oneness.'*

# Vibe 50 Clear intentions

Your voice is powerful and it is heard. Even if you have difficulties speaking or are deaf, know that your voice is loud, powerful and heard by the divine.

The voice I'm talking about isn't just the sound that comes from your mouth, it's the intentions that you hold within you. Every single one of your intentions goes out into the universe and comes back to you like a boomerang – especially if you focus on it. So it's important for you to think about what you desire and love, rather than what you fear. You need to get clear about what you want. You may feel drawn to creating lists, either on paper or in your mind, about what you would like to do – but if you know for a fact that in the past they've become lists of what you *haven't* achieved, it's time to change that.

You have an endless source of inspiration and light within you. However, if you feel that a particular goal or aspiration is 'unrealistic', chances are you aren't going to create it. But no miracle or manifestation is bigger than the next. Nothing is unrealistic unless it is unrealistic in your own mind – if your intentions dim when you think about a dream, then that's what's going to come to fruition.

## Vibe of the day

You are encouraged to get crystal clear about your intentions. What is it you want from life? What does it feel realistic for you to create? You are only limited by your capacity to accept miracles. Today encourage yourself to go beyond the limits of your past and move into a space of unlimited potential.

Think about a goal or goals that you are ready to manifest. Be clear that these intentions are realistic and within your grasp. Realize that you have the capacity to bring them into reality.

*'I have the right to be heard.*

*The universe listens to my intentions.*

*Today I choose to be clear about what I want.*

*I have the capacity to create miracles.*

*I choose to welcome those miracles with open arms!*

*And so it is!'*

#ShareYourVibe

*'The universe is always listening. I make my intentions clear.'*

# SEE

*Chakra:* Ajna (brow/third eye)

*Location:* The centre of the forehead

*Colour:* Indigo/purple

*Element:* Space

*Ajna* is a Sanskrit word that means 'perceive' or 'perception'. It is the name of the spiritual energy centre that is related to our inner vision. It's from this space that clairvoyance is activated and also the ability to see a vision of what we would like to create. If the

Ajna chakra were in nature, it would be the universal life-force, the web of energy that moves through all of life, bringing a sense of connection to all that is.

This energy centre is all about the head, the eyes and everything that goes on in the mind. It governs how we see the world and how we process all that we experience in the world.

All that we see on the outside is ultimately an expression of what we believe on the inside, so as you move into the Ajna-centre lessons you learn to shift your mindset from fear to love. Here you also recognize that mindfulness is taking the time to acknowledge and process all that's in your mind.

## *Vibe 51* Daydream to the extreme

When I was at school I was known for daydreaming. I could easily sit for hours on end just gazing into space – much to my teachers' disapproval. Although it appeared to the outside world that I was doing absolutely nothing, in my inner world I was having the time of my life.

To this day I dream up the most amazing journeys. Even if my eyes are open I don't always see what's going on in the outside world because I'm off on my own little inner adventures.

I believe daydreaming is the key to awakening and developing the inner vision. When you daydream, you give permission for your third eye to open. That is the space in your spiritual anatomy that allows you to connect to heaven, angels, guides and even your ability to manifest.

If you were told off for daydreaming when you were younger, either by your parents or your teachers, there's a chance you'll feel it's a bad thing or a waste of time. It's time to realize that it's actually a miracle. Daydreaming is a powerful tool that allows you to access your deepest state of consciousness, strengthen it and allow it to come through more clearly into your daily life.

In the space of your mind you have the capacity to create miracles. Remember a miracle is a shift of perception. It's the ability to think about the best possible outcome of a situation rather than plan for failure. A miracle is the moment when you fall out with someone and you imagine them being surrounded by healing light rather than imagining you are punching them or throwing daggers at them.

You can create miracles. You are worthy of miracles. Now make miracles.

## Vibe of the day

Today you are encouraged to daydream to the extreme. Find the time to go off on a little adventure somewhere. Your eyes can be open or closed. Maybe you'll dedicate your daydream to service to others by imagining all the people you love or work with being helped and supported by angels. Or you can imagine yourself doing your favourite sport. Or you can relive a childhood memory or hobby. Whatever it is, do something that makes you feel alive. And as your daydreams get clearer, your psychic vision will too.

Just to make it even easier for you, here's an intention to release old blocks surrounding dreaming:

*'It is my spiritual right to dream.*

*I give myself full permission to create experiences in my mind.*

*My mind is the medium of miracles and
today I allow it to express itself.*

*Within my dreams I am filled with unlimited potential.*

*I allow that freedom to wash over my entire life.*

*Dreaming allows my inner vision to be expressed.*

*I am a dreamer and that's a great thing!'*

#ShareYourVibe
*'Through daydreaming I strengthen
my connection to miracles!'*

# Vibe 52 Inner vision, outer expression

What you see in your inner world has a lot to do with what you experience in your outer world. So you need to craft thoughts, dreams and ideas that work for you in a loving way.

It's important to say that this isn't about controlling the universe. It's more about meeting it halfway and allowing it to support you.

How it works, as we've already mentioned, is that every idea, vision, dream and feeling that happens on the inside has some sort of impression on the field that surrounds you. You know when one thing goes wrong and it gets you down, you keep thinking about it and then the day just gets worse and worse?

It's in the moments of doubt, loss and confusion that you need to grasp and assert your inner vision more than ever.

## Vibe of the day

Today you are encouraged to craft your inner vision. Choose thoughts, feelings and daydreams that work for you. Know that every vision you have is taken out into the universe and is creating your next experience.

If a vision, thought or feeling slips through today that you know isn't working in your favour, you can say something like: 'I cancel that intention and replace it with love!' Then think about something that is working for you.

We all make mistakes, especially with our mind, but know that you can correct this and restate your intentions.

### #ShareYourVibe
'My outer world is an expression of my intentions.'

## Vibe 53 'I am ready to see'

There's a lot of information out there that says being clairvoyant or psychic or even seeing angels is only for 'the gifted'. This is an illusion created by the ego because people don't want others to be as 'special' as they are.

The truth is we are all special and we are all gifted. For that reason none of us is more special and none of us is more gifted than anyone else. Sure, we all have our talents and are able to do some things better than others, but I like to kick spiritual élitism in the butt.

It is your spiritual right to see spirit because *you are spirit*. The fact that you are a soul living in a body guarantees that you can recognize, connect to and develop the ability to see your true self.

If you are ready to see on a soul level – if you would like to see your guides, angels or anything else in a spiritual context – then you must be willing to acknowledge and accept your own light first. It is through the acknowledgement of your own true essence and the honouring of your soul that you will develop your spiritual vision.

# Vibe of the day

It's time to acknowledge that you are a higher energy living in a physical body. You are a soul having a human experience.

✦ Go to the mirror and look directly into your eyes.

✦ See the light inside your eyes.

✦ See that there is an eternal love behind those eyes.

✦ Gaze lovingly into those eyes and know they are the mirror of your soul.

✦ When you are ready, set this intention:

> '*I am ready to see the light of my soul.*
> *I am ready to see who I truly am.*
> *I am ready to see this light in all of humanity.*

*I am ready to see.*
*And so it is!'*

✦ Enjoy this moment. Breathe it out. Know that you are creating deep shifts in your vision.

*#ShareYourVibe*
*'It is my spiritual right to see*
*the light of my soul!'*

# *Vibe 54* VIP – very important perception

Perception is everything. As we've just seen, how you perceive things influences how you experience them. You are now in a space of awakening a vision that is sacred.

The third-eye centre is found in the centre of the forehead and it is in this space that our inner vision is activated. Its name, *Ajna*, is the Sanskrit for 'perception' and this chakra is known within Indian spiritual texts as the one that acts as a bridge linking students to their guru, or teacher. It also allows us to connect to our inner teacher.

Whenever you focus on a certain aspect of your physical body, you send energy in that direction. If you meditate on the middle of your forehead, just above your brows, you will send streams of energy to your third eye.

This is an important aspect of enhancing your spiritual perception because you are taking the opportunity to acknowledge a divine aspect of yourself that may have lain dormant for many years. If you would like to see more, visualize better and open up your connection to the other side, this is something that requires your attention.

# Vibe of the day

Today you are encouraged to bring your attention to your third-eye centre. Doing a short meditation while bringing all of your awareness to the space between your brows will allow divine energy to flow freely to this space.

Generally the best way to do it is sitting up in a seated or cross-legged position. If you find it difficult to do this while bringing your attention to your third eye, another great way to do the meditation is to lie down and place something light on your forehead. When I learned this technique in India we did it with a one-rupee coin (we actually did it seated, so had to master keeping the coin on our forehead), but I recommend using a small crystal of your choice. A ring is another suggestion.

✦ Once you've figured out how you're going to conduct the meditation, sit or lie down.

✦ Allow your breathing to become steady and deep. If you're lying down, it's a good idea to keep your energy engaged (so you don't sleep) by drawing in your solar plexus (belly) a little.

✦ Imagine that with each and every breath you draw in, a pure white light is moving through your whole body and arriving at the space between your brows.

✦ To work on developing your visual skills you can say, either internally or out loud, something like:

*'With each and every breath I draw the light of the universe into my inner vision!'*

✦ Do this meditation for as long as you feel you need. I recommend setting a timer for 5–10 minutes, but it can be longer if you're getting more comfortable with sitting in meditation.

#ShareYourVibe
*'I am ready to experience my inner vision.'*

# Vibe 55 All-seeing eye

The chakra wheels often look like vortices or spinning wheels, but the third eye always stands out because it is often seen as an actual eye.

In Eastern traditional artwork (both Hindu and Buddhist) you will see many of the deities with a third eye literally sitting between their brows. Often this eye isn't fully open. You can actually open and close your third eye at will, but it will also open and close very naturally during your life.

Although there isn't an actual eyeball sitting between your brows, the energy of this chakra will allow you to picture it that way, so that you can look deeply into it to create a connection with it and even activate its abilities.

Seeing my third-eye centre has been one of the most exciting aspects of my personal spiritual development. I feel this centre has always craved my attention. Ever since I was a kid I've drawn eyes on scrap paper and for many years I had recurring headaches right in the middle of my head.

# Vibe of the day

Today you are encouraged to look into your third-eye centre. There are many options for doing this. If you are a visual person, a meditation is the best place to start, but if you are highly creative, you can paint or draw your third eye so you can see it on a physical level.

I recommend you try this meditation. With it you can create a really personal relationship with your third eye and therefore your inner vision and your psychic abilities.

✦ Set up your space in whatever way feels good to you. You may want to bring in crystals and light some candles. Do what feels right – less or more.

✦ Sit quietly and take several deep breaths to centre yourself.

✦ Then set this intention:

*'Divine sacred vision, Ajna, third eye, brow chakra,*

*I am ready to awaken.*

*I am ready to experience my truth.*

*Thank you for revealing your true essence to me so that I can understand how to love and nurture you better.*

*I recognize that you are a divine aspect of me.*

*I am sorry for the times I have ignored your prompts, your guidance and your vision. Today I am ready to change that.*

*I am ready to embrace your light fully. I am willing to see through you.*

*I choose now to see my third eye.'*

✦ Take a deep breath then close your physical eyes.

✦ Visualize your third-eye centre. What does it look like? What colour is it? Is it vertically placed or is it horizontal, like your physical eyes? Does it have anything within it? What is it allowing you to see?

✦ When you are ready, thank it for letting you see it.

✦ Open your eyes.

✦ Note down anything you received.

✦ Now go and enjoy your day with clear new vision.

#ShareYourVibe
*'My inner vision is a divine aspect of myself.'*

# *Vibe 56* Mindful manifesto

Mindfulness is the key to inner vision. Most people have the crazy idea that practising mindfulness (which is a new fad) means creating complete silence in their head, but actually it means creating a sense of awareness of your thoughts and feelings. Mindfulness practice starts with something very simple: how you sit. Finding a comfortable sitting position is important in order to increase your sense of mindfulness and connection to your inner vision.

Once you're comfortable, be mindful of your mind. You're going to have thoughts. You're going to have crazy thoughts. Shopping lists. Fears. Emotions. Resentful feelings. Loving feelings. Outfits. Who knows what's going to come into your mind when you sit down to meditate?

Instead of trying to silence your thoughts, being mindful means choosing to acknowledge them. Every time a thought comes up that you feel is putting you off your vibe or distracting you from the point of your meditative focus, you can acknowledge it and change it.

But when you start to affirm, 'Aargh, I can't do this – my mind won't shut up,' you are literally setting yourself up for disaster!

## Vibe of the day

Today you are encouraged to find your mindfulness manifesto. You are encouraged to take several breaks in a comfortable sitting position or even when you are walking. Allow your mind to open up wide. Give permission for your thoughts to flow freely.

Every time you have a thought or experience that throws you off-track, just use the affirmation: 'Today I choose to be mindful.'

You can even add specifics on to the end of it, for example:

*'Today I choose to be mindful of the blessings in my life.'*

*'Today I choose to be mindful of the beautiful blue sky!'*

*'Today I choose to be mindful of my fearful thoughts and replace them with loving ones!'*

You get the idea? Now get mindful, my beauty!

#ShareYourVibe
*'Mindfulness is choosing to become aware of your thoughts and feelings.'*

## Vibe 57 Massaging the mind

I don't know about you, but I love having a massage, especially if I've been doing a lot of workouts, travelling or sitting at my desk (all of which happen regularly).

Having the knots and tension taken out of my body can be sore but is always good. I love that feeling of fingers running over my skin as if the divine healing of the universe is pulsing through every cell of my body.

I also love to massage myself with oil, either in the bath or just after the bath, to soothe my muscles after intense yoga workouts.

That feeling of massaging oil into my skin really allows me to give myself the love I deserve.

The mind also craves massage. It craves the same release of tension and knots that our body craves. It loves to be given the TLC it deserves.

The mind is a phenomenal space. I like to see it as an altar to the divine, but it's also the place where we make our next move, think about our angels, create our shopping lists and express our feelings.

Your mind is miraculous. Give it a massage today.

## Vibe of the day

You massage your mind every time you meditate – every time you take a moment or two to breathe, go within, become mindful and open your inner vision. You can massage your mind through visualization and prayer too.

Today you are encouraged to call upon your guardian angel to help you give your mind the massage it deserves. As you will say a prayer and then lie down for a nap, it's probably best to do it when you have time for a rest or before you go to bed.

First of all, here's a prayer to your mind:

*'Thank you, mind, for taking some time to relax today.
I realize that sometimes you are overworked and
stressed. I am encouraging you to take some moments
to rest and receive a massage that will help nourish
you and take away anything that's not serving you.'*

And here's a prayer to your guardian angel:

*'Thank you, guardian angel, for stepping forth with
your bright light and healing hands and massaging
my mind. I encourage you to wrap this space
within me in a light of healing, care and love.*

*Thank you for taking any fear or blockages away and for
replacing them with energy that is peaceful and loving.*

*I am now ready to sit back and relax and allow my
mind to be cared for and massaged by you.*

*And so it is!'*

Then take some time to relax, have a nap or go to bed,
knowing your angel is taking care of everything and your mind
is supported and loved.

*#ShareYourVibe*
*'I allow my mind to be massaged
by an angel of light!'*

## Vibe 58 Angel eyes

I have a special phrase and it's really simple:

### *'In order to see angels, you have to be an angel!'*

It's not always easy. But I believe that it is through being kind,
generous and supportive of others that we are able to perceive
angels and understand them at a deeper level.

Angels want nothing more than for us to be happy and supported. They want the whole of humanity to understand that no matter what their race, creed or colour, they are all divine and all equal.

Angels see us all as equal, but they also see us for who we truly are – they see our soul or spirit, the eternal source of love within us. We don't always see it, either in ourselves or in others, especially if they are being challenging or difficult. We don't always see the best in others either, particularly in strangers, because we don't know them and aren't looking for their light.

Angels, on the other hand, see the good in all. They see the soul within all of humanity. They look for our loving essence and they encourage us to embrace it.

From the moment you were born your angel has seen your light and been waiting for you to discover it. When you see that light in yourself and then in others too, you are awakening a vision that is sacred and holding the space for others to discover their own miraculous light.

# Vibe of the day

If you are ready to awaken your inner vision, you must lift the vibration of your vision. So today you are encouraged to see through the eyes of angels.

Wherever you are, wherever you go and whatever you do today, acknowledge that everyone you see, no matter who they are or what they are doing, has a soul within them and that soul is ready to be lit up.

If you can see that light then their energy will vibrate at a higher level and you yourself will move into a space that is wise, compassionate and loving.

# Vibe 59 The lamp of knowledge

There's an amazing quote that I came across while researching inner vision and it came from the Bible (Matthew 6:22):

> *'The eye is the lamp of the body; so then if your eye is clear, your whole body will be full of light.'*

Your third eye is a lamp of knowledge. It's the space within you that helps you move into and embrace your light body. Your light body is the true you, it's your soul body, and when you really acknowledge, understand and accept that light within you, everything that seems separate from you will be restored to you.

I've learned through my study of the Indian spiritual texts the Tantras, Vedas and Upanishads that the third eye is the most sacred of the chakras because it's the space where all the different aspects of the spiritual anatomy join together. It's where masculine and feminine energy join to create a sense of oneness and a connection to the soul, and that's why we are able to perceive soul energy, vibrational energy and the divine from this space.

What I'm basically saying is when we repair all the other chakras (as we've been doing in the last 50 or so lessons), we allow the energy of our soul self and the divine to move through our entire spiritual DNA.

As mentioned earlier, energy flows from Muladhara, the root chakra, at the base of the spine up through the rest of the chakras via the Sushumna channel, while masculine and feminine energy, known as Pingala and Ida, crisscross each other as they rise to the top of the six major chakras and join at the third-eye centre:

*Energy moving up through the chakras.*

# Vibe of the day

It's time to activate your lamp of knowledge. Today, set your intention to activate your third-eye centre in order to access, accept and express the vibes that move through you, with the words:

*'Thank you, universe, for allowing divine energy to move through my spiritual anatomy and to meet as one at my third-eye centre. It feels so good to know that I am at the point in my spiritual practice where I am unlocking my inner vision.*

*I am now ready to activate and accept the clarity of my inner vision.*

*Thank you, universe, for sending angels, guides and any other support into my life that will help me fully embrace my inner vision. It feels so good to trust this divine and holy aspect of myself. I am ready to see clearly now and I'm grateful that you are helping me do this!'*

Recognize that over the days of doing this spiritual work you have raised your vibration considerably and from this point onwards the more time you spend working on these exercises, the clearer your inner vision and wisdom will be.

### #ShareYourVibe
*'I choose to see the light clearly!'*

# Vibe 60 Opening your third eye!

Your chakras open and close – they interact with the energy that moves around them. They are amazing spaces that naturally move with you and your flow in life. When it comes to the third eye, you can choose when to open it and when to close it. This freedom gives you the space to relax your mind and focus it when you need to.

When the third eye is open, all of the spiritual energy in your spinal column moves upwards and meets there, giving you spiritual strength and the energy to see. When you open up your third eye, it's like putting on clairvoyant sunglasses.

I highly recommend taking time to sit in your spiritual practice and open your third eye, because it allows you to get used to the energy of that chakra. Many people, especially if they've been encouraged to stay quiet about their visions and dreams, find this exercise liberating and emotional. There is a sense of freedom because you are actualizing a deeper aspect of yourself and recognizing something that may have been long forgotten. The emotions come because you are releasing old fears and traumas that have been pushed into this space.

When I began to exercise my third eye and give it the permission it required to open up and express itself fully, I had experiences that were both transcendental and emotional. During my meditations I had visions of angels, saints and ascended masters. I also saw fear and trauma leave my body.

One particular memory was seeing all my old schoolteachers pointing at me. When I went into my dream states in class, the teachers would shout at me, telling me to 'concentrate'. When they did this, they would point directly at the space between my brows and it would feel as if they were physically hurting me. To this day I tell people never to point at me. I believe the energy in anger can be felt and held, especially by the intuitive chakras. I was finally able to release the energy of my school experiences through deep meditation.

There may be old memories or fears hidden in your third-eye chakra and this is all the more reason to open it. The memories contained in it could be standing between you and you capacity to see and interact with heavenly love.

# Vibe of the day

Today choose to set some time aside to work on opening and clearing your third eye. This process may sound simple, but can be extremely effective, especially if you've followed all of the techniques that have come before it.

✦ When you're ready, settle down in a comfortable space in which it's safe for you to release any emotions.

✦ Set the intention:

> *'Thank you, universal life-force, for surrounding me in a space of protection.*
>
> *I am ready to awaken and activate my third-eye centre.*
>
> *Thank you, angels of light, for removing any blocks, trauma and fear that stand between me and my inner vision.*
>
> *I am ready to see on a psychic and spiritual level.*
>
> *I am ready to perceive heavenly love.'*

✦ Close your eyes and move into a restful meditation.

✦ Imagine/visualize that between your brows your third eye is opening. You may see a physical eye opening up or even a doorway. (Whatever works for you is right.)

✦ Feel that your energy is rising high and you are drawing choirs of angels and heavenly love towards you.

✦ Spend as long as you need in this space. Be aware of anything that is being released. The universe will handle this for you. Relax and allow your clairvoyance to refocus.

# #ShareYourVibe
*'I trust my inner vision!'*

# KNOW

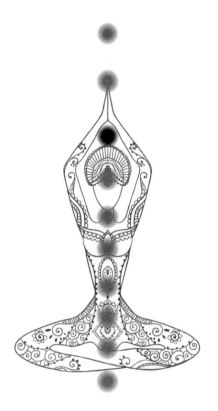

*Chakra:* Sahasrara (crown)

*Location:* The crown

*Colour:* Violet/white

*Elements:* All

*Sahasrara* is a Sanskrit word that means '1,000-petalled' and as the name of the crown chakra it refers to the idea that this chakra is an energetic lotus with 1,000 petals. The crown chakra governs our spiritual connection and allows us to process and channel our interaction with the divine. If it were in nature it would be creation itself – the energy that creates the soil, the rain, the sun and the air. It would be everything that is.

The crown centre allows us to use our divine connection and our sense of connection to the world. The more time we spend in deep meditation and spiritual study, accepting who we are, the more it opens up. This centre also governs our brain, our memory, our academic ability and emotional intelligence and our awareness of the spiritual realms.

As we work on the crown chakra and allow our 1,000 lotus petals to open, we allow ourselves to heal any challenges we have with the divine and our spiritual connection.

## *Vibe 61* No separation

You are really progressing along your spiritual pathway. If there were a sixth gear you would have just moved into it and you are allowing yourself to be more attuned than ever.

As your DSP grows and you become more spiritually aware, sometimes it is very easy to forget about the foundations of your pathway. You are a bright light in the world and the universe is grateful for you. You are shining and being the positive force in the room wherever you are, but it's important to remember that you aren't doing this without support.

You've endured fear and encountered loss and the feeling of being physically separate from the people you love. That isn't an easy aspect of your path and you have felt the pain of it. But, although you've had those feelings and encountered the hurt, the truth is that separation is just a temporary illusion.

The reason the feeling of being separate and lost is an illusion is because it isn't love. Only love is real. Those you have lost, both from the Earth and those you have separated from in life, will always be with you.

If you could imagine an amazing universe right now with beautiful stars shining brightly, you would see they were all connected in some way because they were all sharing the universe – they were all individual facets of one great and beautiful picture. In fact that is who you are – a facet of beautiful light – and your presence here adds to the beauty of this universe.

If you've been feeling lost or separate, know that this is old energy coming up and coming out so that you can replace it with thoughts, feelings, beautiful memories and affirmations that are echoing your truth.

# Vibe of the day

'I am a divine facet of the universe.

It feels so good to know I am never separate from love.

The love in my heart connects me to all those I love.

I awaken the memory in my mind that allows
me to feel connected with all that is.

Thank you, universe, for helping me realize there is
no time, distance or space between me and love.

I am love.'

# #ShareYourVibe
'I am part of the bigger picture. I am the universe!'

 **Vibe 62** **Feeling life-force**

Life-force runs through your veins. It passes through every major organ of your body. It flows through the animals and vegetables of the planet. It moves through everything that is. It is powerful, magical and real. It is your connection to love, to wisdom, to the angels, to healing and to the universe.

Life-force is yours. You deserve to know it. You are running on it now. Feeling it is natural. You sometimes need some imagination to do that, but it's there and you can tap into the beat and wave running through you.

If you have ever seen the movie *Avatar* (and if you haven't, you need to), you will remember that there is a subtle life-force that runs through all of the avatars, their plants, animals and land. All of this energy is connected to the force of being that they call Eywa. This is so similar to what clairvoyants see and to the level of connectivity we can reach when we move into our meditation practice.

There are a few things that have really helped me develop my awareness of life-force. One of them is being aware of my breath. In yoga, the breath represents *prana*, or life-force. I decided to become conscious of my breath, especially while meditating, doing angel work and on my yoga mat. Now I am aware that as I draw in air, I am drawing in the *prana* or life-force that surrounds me.

I have also allowed myself to imagine that this life-force is moving through all of the people I meet. And I ask myself questions while I'm gazing at my cat. For instance, I'll say things like: 'If the life-force of Ralph were to be seen by the physical eye right now, what would it look like?' I then picture it in my mind and allow my eyes to develop this awareness.

I believe that when used correctly, imagination can be the doorway to developing spiritual awareness.

## Vibe of the day

Realize that everyone and everything you see today has life-force moving through it. If you find it difficult to visualize or see, don't worry, because you can feel it.

For every living person and every living animal or plant you see today, say to yourself: 'There is life-force running through this [person/animal/plant] and I am willing to see and feel it!'

The more you affirm this, the more you are able to connect to this natural phenomenon that surrounds you.

**#ShareYourVibe**
*'There is a life-force moving through all living things.'*

## Vibe 63 Soul shifting

Your soul is the purest aspect of who you are. It is known as your light body, spirit, higher self and even your 'true self'. The soul has a greater sense of awareness than the body – it contains memories and information that you are able to access.

When you begin to make shifts on a soul level, it doesn't mean you have to lose all sense of awareness of the outer world and it doesn't mean you have to float around on a fluffy cloud either. In fact, the more time you spend becoming aware of your soul and acknowledging it, the greater the sense of integration, connection and development you will feel.

There is a true sense of integration that is taking place at this time. You are recognizing that love is all there is – it's something you've felt for a long time. At the same time you are on your human journey, working on doing your best and being the best person you can possibly be with the knowledge and information you have.

The reason you are drawn to healing, angels and raising your vibration is because your soul has had the opportunity to express itself. When you find people of the same mindset, idea or beliefs, you will feel a deep soul recognition.

You are at a point on your own path where you have seen great healing occur. A profound process of growth has occurred within you and the universe is celebrating with you.

## Vibe of the day

Today you are encouraged to acknowledge the growth that's taken place in you and the new awareness you are bringing to your life.

Take time to sit and acknowledge that you are more positive than you've ever been, you're more aware than you've ever been and it's going to keep getting better from here on in.

Here are some suggestions to help you:

✦ Share via prayer your gratitude for your inner strength.

✦ Write in a journal about the changes you've made.

✦ Dance to your favourite song to celebrate your transformations. Just do whatever makes you feel *alive*!

✦ Thank your creator and angels for getting you where you are today!

#ShareYourVibe
*'I am so grateful for the changes I've made in myself and in my life!'*

# Vibe 64 Spring-clean your aura

Your aura is the field of energy that projects from your spiritual body. It is affected by your state of mind, how balanced your chakras are and the environment to which you are exposed.

Your aura is always changing and evolving. You will hear about people being told their aura colour by intuitive mediums and so on, but what they were told then is probably different now.

There's no such thing as a bad aura. People worry about this, but it's a myth. There's no way you can have a bad aura, but there will be people who have energy that yours doesn't recognize or agree with. As I've said before, when you see someone you love or meet someone who has similar interests, or you meet someone and feel that you've known them forever, it's a soul recognition. And when you feel the opposite, your intuition is basically saying the person you are meeting isn't for you and they aren't part of your tribe.

Although you can't have a bad aura, there are times when your energy can become cloudy, or what I call 'murky'. It happens when you've been exposed to an energy that isn't in resonance with you, for example when you visit a place and the energy feels 'off', or you've just been in a heated or stressful situation, or you've had an encounter with someone who is challenging and you feel a 'jaggy' energy coming from them. It's time to learn the technique for spring-cleaning your aura.

# Vibe of the day

This technique can come in very handy. Do it now and anytime you feel the need to give your aura a nice once-over, even if you have to go to the bathroom for five minutes to get some privacy. It's quick, effective and relieving.

You can stand or sit to do this.

✦ Hold your hands up, palms facing upwards.

✦ Close your eyes and imagine you are collecting the pure light of the universe in your hands.

✦ Open your eyes. Then, using your hands as a sweeper, run them all the way round your aura and all the way down your chakras. Imagine that you have a magical brush of light in your hands and as you comb through your aura with your fingers, all sense of stagnancy, blockage and negativity is being released.

✦ You can then say something like: 'My energy field is positively clear and full of light!'

✦ Then heave a sigh of relief!

> #ShareYourVibe
> 'I clear my energy of any energetic
> clutter and it feels so good!'

# Vibe 65 Opening your crown

The crown chakra is the chakra with the purest energy available. This opening just above the head is described as a lotus flower and is related to our divine connection and our deepest knowing. It's the space where we draw down from the universe support, love and guidance. This spectacular energy centre, which is between violet and pure crystal in colour, is the most unlikely of all to get contaminated or become unbalanced, but it is possible.

The crown chakra is generally always open on some level, even if just a little. But if we've fallen away from spirituality, fallen out with Source or decided that there's nothing else out there after our human life, we've generally closed off this space.

Although it may not be an intentional thing, this 'lonely' or 'helpless' attitude can really create a sense of disconnection from the universe. It's something that all of us have felt at some point – and sometimes it's needed in order to prompt us to reclaim our strength and the power to change what we need to.

With self-empowerment, hope, faith and trust, the lotus of your crown begins to open up, and that's when the wonder of life comes back in again. You can choose to open that space in order to feel connected, loved and supported by the power we call the creator.

# Vibe of the day

Use this intention to open your crown chakra and allow the support of the universe to flow freely into your world:

*'There is an energy within me
represented by 1,000 petals.*

*I allow this energy to bloom, I give permission
for my connection to soar.*

*As I open up to receive the love and
support of creation I deserve,*

*I become a light of inspiration,
creativity and productivity.*

*I am ready to feel connected, I am ready
to know my source and I am ready to allow
that source to flow through me with ease.*

*My chakras are aligned and charged, my
connection is open and strong.*

*It feels so good to know that the presence
of light I seek is within me now and
forever more. Today I choose to see that
light. Today I choose to shine that light.*

*And so it is!'*

You may want to sit and receive for a little while after this intention or, if you're on the move, just allow the download to happen as you go.

# Vibe 66 Getting good with God

There's a good chance that on your spiritual path you've had a few challenging moments with the word 'God' or, even more so, the idea of that presence.

There are many religions, beliefs, ideas and teachings in this world. Many cross-reference one another, while others completely contradict one another. I've purposely avoided using the word 'God' up to now in this book because it's a word that puts off many people and that many associate with fear, trauma and torment.

If you're good with God and the word 'God', then great, you'll swim through this lesson (but please bear with me). If you're not, I'm so glad to have you here.

In order for you to move to a higher vibration and shine more brightly on your own spiritual pathway, it's good to get over any negative ideas you have about the divine. You are encouraged to know that whatever torments or traumas you've had with 'God', or people's idea of God, none of them have been real. God is just a word. Source or the universe (which is just another word for God) isn't a man, isn't a religion, isn't a dogma and isn't a set of rules to tell you who, what or how to be.

The universe is a presence of love which desires nothing from you. It gives you its full permission to live your life the way you want to live it. It places no expectations on you and there's no punishment coming your way if you don't make it to church or your meditation mat this weekend – absolutely nothing.

Whatever you've read, been told or threatened with is just someone's opinion. The truth is, if you've been told something fearful, it's just someone's way of trying to control you or get you to conform to their way of thinking. It's not real. Only love is real.

# Vibe of the day

*'Today I choose to leave behind all fear regarding the divine.*

*I lovingly release all false claims, power trips, traumas and warnings.*

*I am ready to move beyond the limitations of others' dogma and religion.*

*I realize that the source of our creation is a presence of love.*

*This presence will do nothing to harm me,*

*Nor has it punished me in this lifetime.*

*In every experience I encounter, I have a choice.*

*Today I choose love and to accept the love of the divine.*

*I now allow love to be the force that guides me as I leave behind all that no longer serves me, my spiritual growth or my purpose, which is to be happy.*

*I am free!*

*And so it is!'*

# #ShareYourVibe
*'The source of creation is unconditional love.'*

# Vibe 67 Wisdom is within

Knowledge is something you learn. Wisdom comes from within. Why does it lie within? That's where the divine energy called your soul is, and your soul allows you to receive wisdom, guidance and support on your spiritual path.

You have countless opportunities to open up to heaven and receive that support. It may not always be as easy as it sounds, but dedication and commitment to your path will allow you to access the sacred support of your creator.

The universe put you here to have a fulfilled, exciting and happy life. You weren't born to be poor in any way. You were given the amazing opportunity to come to Earth to learn, grow and remember that love is the only aspect of you that will live for eternity.

Hopefully by this point you've reached a state of positivity and happiness. It's important to remember that what you are moving through right now is a process, and that process is going to take time. You are lifting your energy higher as you focus on growth, positivity, healing and love. As you do so, all the aspects of your life that aren't aligned with that energy (people, places and situations) will find a way of working their way out of your life, and this can be challenging.

It's important to know that you have support within and around you all the time and you can check in with it anytime for that much-needed guidance and insight.

# *Vibe of the day*

Today, check in with the universe throughout your day.

✦ Say:

> *'Thank you, universe, for revealing
> to me what I need to know!'*

✦ Sit or stand with the intention of receiving divine guidance for a few moments.

✦ Then return to your day.

✦ Do this several times.

Your guidance may not arrive in the way you think, but be aware that you are open to receiving wisdom from the soul voice at this time.

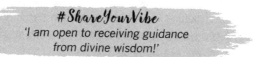

*#ShareYourVibe*
*'I am open to receiving guidance
from divine wisdom!'*

# *Vibe 68* Intuition says, '*No!*'

You get direct hits from your intuition all the time. You know you do, because you say stuff like 'I should have just listened to myself!'

The truth is we're all guilty of ignoring our intuition from time to time. I personally avoided listening in for many years, but recently made a huge breakthrough when I was doing bodywork and healing. After I'd lost around 36kg (80lb) of unneeded body weight, my intuition became clearer and I created an amazing connection to what my body liked and needed.

One day I was at an author party in London with my publisher and there was food and drink on tap – any kind of wine you'd like. Waiters were walking around with all different kinds of fried food and I could see my greedy side coming out, even though I'd just had a beautiful vegan risotto for dinner and I wasn't hungry.

Anyway, the waiter approaches me with this food and my greedy side is desperate for a bit. I can feel my fingers rubbing together and hear a voice inside screaming, 'Don't do it! Don't do it! You're just going to use this as an excuse to sabotage yourself! Don't doooo it!' And at the same time the voice of greed is going, 'Is it tempura? Oh, what sauce can we dip that baby in?'

All of a sudden a huge battle starts to take place in my head and the strangest thing is that I am now a witness to it. I know I don't need it and I know the voice of greed is just trying to get in the way, so I scream out: 'Intuition says, "*No!!!*"'

The waiter gets the idea. Greed goes quiet. I walk away feeling empowered. And my friends give me a high five.

# Vibe of the day

What's your intuition saying 'no' to?

Today you are encouraged to use the affirmation: 'Intuition says, "No!"'

Drop this line anytime you feel urged to say 'no' but can feel a battle going on in your head. It will feel like freedom!

# Vibe 69 Altar to the divine

Having a physical space in which to honour the divine has become an integral part of my life. Although having spiritual statues and crystals aren't going to make you any more spiritual than you already are, having a physical space in your home or office that represents unconditional love helps to keep your vibes high.

When I was growing up I had an interest in different religions and I created an altar quite quickly. It had pagan artwork, crystals, Ganesh (the Indian elephant god) and other spiritual bits and bobs on it. I'd keep my angel cards there and a lil' pile of books that I loved.

Nowadays my whole life has spiritual altars in it. The living space of my home has an altar with Hindu statues and a framed photo of His Holiness the Dalai Lama. My bedroom is literally a spiritual grotto – I've covered the TV on the wall with a scarf (because I never use it) and have a huge statue of Ganesh on an altar, crystals next to my bed and a *Star Wars* Wookie there too to bring balance! As a rule I keep only spiritual books in my bedroom because books carry a vibration too – spiritual ones definitely have a higher vibe than horror stories!

Altars don't have to be fancy. They can be simple areas with photos of loved ones, flowers, crystals or whatever else you feel represents love, positivity and a sense of connection to the divine.

I believe our altar is a physical representation of our mind and whatever we lay upon it we are offering in our mind to the divine. For me, one great example is Ganesh, who is the Hindu deity for removing obstacles. When he sits on my altar I allow my mind to be free of obstacles.

Now when I travel I take a few spiritual items with me to jazz up my hotel-room side-table or the table on stage when I'm speaking. It's a beautiful ritual to have.

# Vibe of the day

✦ Create a space somewhere to honour the divine. If you already have a space, give it a spruce-up.

✦ Collect together photos, flowers, candles, pictures, crystals or whatever helps you honour the divine. Think statues and anything else that you know is all about love.

✦ Clear a space and create your altar to the divine.

✦ Go to this space anytime you feel you've lost your high vibe. Go there to give thanks, to mark your progress, to say your prayers or whenever you need a hit of love. Know this space represents your inner power.

#ShareYourVibe
*'I dress the altar of my mind and know the divine is with me there!'*

# Vibe 70 Synchronicity

Everything happens for a reason. You've heard that a million times, right? But when something goes wrong, it's a difficult phrase to understand.

A lot of people believe that God or the universe is the type of energy that punishes people and even punishes the world. You'll hear people talk about 'acts of God' or be angry with God because 'he' took away someone or something from them.

Synchronicity isn't about saying 'Everything happens for a reason' and it isn't about finding out what that reason is. It's more the universe sending signs to us when we've started to align with divine truth. It's the universe seeing when we're distressed or disconnected and sending out a signal to say it's coming to help. It's the energy of hope coming in and filling us up. It's a reminder that there isn't light at the end of the tunnel – it's the light within us that lights up our way. When we remember our true essence, the tunnel is just another illusion!

## Vibe of the day

Today you're encouraged to remember that the universe has got your back. Remind yourself that it's not out to get you, punish you or get even with you. The universe loves you no matter what. The natural laws of cause and effect work themselves out.

Today you have to trust that there's a light within you that will help you move beyond any challenge or tunnel you find yourself in. Then say:

*'I trust life as it flows with divine timing.'*

#ShareYourVibe
*'Synchronicity is a signal to know the universe has heard your call.'*

# LIGHT UP!

*Chakras:* Earth star and soul star

*Locations:* Earth star: 15–30 centimetres (6–12 inches) below the feet; soul star: 15–30 centimetres (6–12 inches) above the head

*Colours:* Copper (Earth star) and magenta (soul star)

*Elements:* All

The Earth star and soul star chakras help us take our spiritual connection to the next level. The Earth star is the spiritual anchor that holds us deep in the wisdom of Mother Earth. The soul star is the spiritual energy centre that allows us to deepen our connection to the wisdom of the cosmos. When these centres are opened and connected at the same time, we are held by heaven and Earth in perfect balance and perfect trust.

Mother Earth was here well before us – she's millions of years old and she's still going to be here when our physical body has left. When we take the time to acknowledge the Divine Mother and connect with her through the Earth star, we are able to draw up information and guidance from her that will give us a greater sense of connection to the planet and direction in our life.

The universe is the heart of truth and within that energy is age-old wisdom and love that goes beyond our understanding. When we access the soul star, which is seen as a beautiful three-dimensional star of light, we are able to take our spiritual knowledge to the next level.

The lessons and techniques that follow provide spiritual tools that make space within your energy system for upgrades of energy and information. Get ready to release karma, connect to the cosmos and anchor yourself to the Earth!

## *Vibe 71* Cutting the cords

Archangel Michael is the most famous of the angels. He's the one who made it to Hollywood – no joke either! He's known as the saint of protection and is the angelic being who is dedicated to detaching the world from fear. Most images of Michael show him holding a sword made of fire and light, which is a powerful symbol of his ability to cut through fear and liberate us from it.

Michael's name means 'He who is like God' and he is represented by a bright blue light. Anyone can call on him and any of the archangels because, like us, they are ultimately energy, and because they have no physical form they can be in many places at one time. This means Michael is multi-dimensional.

When it comes to challenging and emotionally draining situations, Michael is able to help us because the psychic idea is that they attach to us via cords. Many psychics are actually able to see cords connecting our aura to a person, place, situation or energy. If you've ever had an ex-partner or old friend who just seems to get on your nerves and drain you, there's probably an emotional cord between you that's preventing you from moving forwards. Cords can also link you to places like church, work and goodness knows where else that might drain you. They are also created when you feel someone leeching onto you – on an energetic level they are doing it quite literally, even if they don't realize it.

It's very easy to remove these cords, but many of us don't realize they're there. For that reason it is a great idea to cut them regularly in order to keep your energy pure and clean. When you call on Michael, he comes forth and removes them – but he allows the cords of love to remain.

# Vibe of the day

Today you cut the energetic cords that aren't serving you. Remember, the cords that connect you to your loved ones will always remain, it's just the rest that need to go.

It's easy to do with this simple prayer, and to make it more effective you can imagine an angel of blue light coming and cutting the cords with his sword:

Light up!

'Thank you, Archangel Michael, for
cutting the cords that bind me to
people, places, situations and fear.

I release the weight of the world from my shoulders.

I am safe and free.

And so it is!'

#ShareYourVibe
'Thank you, Archangel Michael,
for keeping me safe!'

## Vibe 72 Spiritual healing

Archangel Raphael is the angel whose name means 'God heals'.
He is the divine physician who is dedicated to the healing of the
world and all the people and animals in it. He is also the angel that
supports people who are on a journey – he's great for helping us
stay healthy and happy while we're travelling.

Healing energy is a light that can enter your body and life. When
you ask the angels for healing, they will of course bring that to you,
but, like all things, they can only bring you as much as you feel is
able to reach you.

Angels are unlimited beings, as are we, but our human level of
intelligence can allow us to feel there is a limit on the number of
miracles that can happen in our life. When I first learned that we
could ask angels for help, I would pray to them for healing and I
soon realized that a lot of my requests were met, but many weren't.

I meditated deeply on this, searching for answers. I knew I had to figure out the best way to pray to angels for healing.

Through angel books, I learned that angels were beings of the present moment. They could help us overcome the past and be our best, but not in the future – it had to be in the present. So I realized that in order for them to help us heal, I had to welcome that healing into the present moment rather than waiting for the future to bring it.

Healing is all about our ability to accept it and to see that the universe and the angels have an unlimited source of it. Try to go beyond your limits and welcome healing into the here and now.

# Vibe of the day

Today you are encouraged to welcome Archangel Raphael and his healing energy into your life. On some level, either mental, emotional, physical or spiritual, healing energy will do you good. There's a good chance you need a boost anyway, and it never hurts to ask for this stuff.

Instead of allowing healing to exist in the future, realize it is happening here and now. It's there for you, just waiting to be accepted into your life. Today you accept it.

*'Thank you, Archangel Raphael, healing angels and anyone else who can help. I welcome your healing light into my body, mind and soul in this present moment. I realize that I deserve to be nourished and I deserve to feel full and well.*

*Thank you, thank you, thank you – my body is the safest place to be on this planet and I allow my vibration to rise in the presence of this healing light. It feels so good to be well from tip to toe. Ah! Welcome healing light, welcome!*

*And so it is!'*

# Vibe 73 Spiritual protection

Cleanse. Tone. Moisturize. You've heard that before, right? Well, that's how I treat my energy. Most people are pretty rubbish (sorry/not sorry to be so blunt) at looking after their energy and I really believe that protecting yourself and your space is critical to progressing spiritually and raising your vibes.

In one-day workshops there's often not too much emphasis on spiritual protection and that disturbs me, because I care about people and I want them to be their best. So pay attention now...

We've all felt drained and under threat when we've been exposed to an energy we haven't resonated with, whether that has been a place or a person, and many of us have learned how to put our shields up, but generally we do it far too late.

I know from personal experience that I've put my shields up only to realize that I've felt more drained afterwards than before. Why? Because I've sealed the energy in. And you've probably done that too.

Here's the game-changer: when you're exposed to an energy you don't vibe with, you have to excuse yourself, go to the bathroom and cut the cords as in vibe 71. Once you've done that, you can put your shields up. If you don't first disconnect from what's causing you distress, you're literally keeping that energy in your force-field and it will feed off you until you are drained, tired and washed out.

# Vibe of the day

Today you are encouraged to cleanse, tone and moisturize your aura.

Here's how it works:

✦ *Cleanse:* You cut your cords to make sure you are free of the energy. Excuse yourself and go to the bathroom if you need to – your energy is more important than manners.

✦ *Tone:* Tell yourself that you are a divine being of light and you are limitless in potential. This raises your vibe high.

✦ *Moisturize:* Call on the universe or your guardian angel, favourite saint or someone in heaven you trust to keep you safe, or imagine a force-field in whatever light you choose surrounding you and your aura.

Get on it. Do your thang. We're this deep in the book now. You know how this stuff works. Carve out your spiritual practice, cleanse your vibes and protect your light. You can do it.

### #ShareYourVibe
*'Feeling safe is my spiritual right.'*

# *Vibe 74* Spiritual nurture

How about some fun? How about expressing your inner child? There are people out there (I've met them) who don't like to have fun because when they were young they were told not to (I hope that wasn't you). I've also met people who have felt really disconnected from their inner child or their own childhood.

It is essential in the raising of your vibes to lift the energy of your inner child. The little you is inside still and essentially we are all children of the universe, learning every day and trying to do our best.

You can spend time working with your inner child and lifting that energy now. It will never be too late – no matter what your age now, or how old you feel, your inner child will never be lost.

The inner child is the part of you that will take things to heart and feel overwhelmed or not good enough. It's the little part of you that doesn't like being told what you're doing is wrong, because it feels like being told off when you were a child.

In order to help heal your inner child or to keep that part of yourself free, filled with love and supported, you can take time to nourish and nurture it in your spiritual practice. Imagine that the six-year-old you is standing by your side and they still have the feeling that they are a 'bad boy' or a 'bad girl' or, even worse, that they aren't 'cool enough' or 'good enough'. Imagine that they just want to be loved.

Even if you were in an extremely loving and nurturing home or family, there's a great chance that the wee you could still be doing with some love. It could be that you grew up fast because you had siblings to help or a sick parent, or that you were bullied all the way through school. Know that what you do now can help you to free that old energy so that you can move forwards in a more focused and fun way.

# Vibe of the day

Today you are encouraged to write a self-love note to your inner child.

✦ Write a detailed letter beginning with 'Dear' and then your name and offering some words of advice, healing and acceptance.

✦ Write about whatever experiences remind you of feeling unloved or not good enough and tell your inner child that no matter what has happened to them, they are going to turn out pretty awesome (because you are awesome right now).

✦ Tell them that they're going to be okay and more importantly that you love them – that you love their hairstyle, clothing and personality. Make them feel loved. Give them some nurturing advice.

✦ Then put your letter in an envelope and seal it.

✦ You can keep this letter in your journal or you can burn it or even plant it. Do whatever you feel you need to do. But make sure you read it back to yourself first.

That's it for today. Intense but good. No excuses. Get it done.

# Vibe 75 Karma releasing

We're getting to the point in your daily spiritual practice where you're ready to amp up your spiritual connection and learn more about the support that's out there for you in this bloomin' amazing universe.

We know about karma – we've discussed it already in this book. We've recognized that it's the spiritual law of cause and effect. When you do something, it has an effect on the next part of your life, because your behaviour is an expression of your point of attraction.

Let's simplify that, even though you've probably already clicked as to what we're saying here. The law of attraction means like attracts like, so your behaviour attracts similar experiences or energy to you.

However, there's another aspect of karma that we haven't talked about: past lives. There are two types: lives we feel we want to leave behind and lives we could be benefiting from in terms of the lessons we're learning now.

We can be born with karma or memories of past lives that influence our point of attraction (sometimes unbeknownst to us) and this can create roadblocks for us even if we don't know about it. Fortunately, we can call on the divine to help us release that old karma and reach a new level of freedom.

I remember once doing a session for someone who had problems having children. I was intrigued, because the doctors she was working with said everything in her body and her partner's body was in full working order and she had come to me as a last resort to work out what was happening on a spiritual level. I remember feeling that what was going on was a past-life trauma or fear that was standing between her and her ability to become a mother.

I tuned in psychically and realized that in a previous life she had been the mother of three children who had been taken away from her. She had gone on to live a sad, lonely life and had been an outcast from society. The fear of losing her children had been reborn with her in this life and this old energy was standing between her and having a child.

When I explained the situation, she said it was if she knew the story already – that somewhere within her there was a 'click' or resonance when she heard it. She wept and let out a lot of built-up emotion.

We were able to clear her karma using prayer and I was pleased to receive a picture of her baby daughter while I was writing this book. It's really amazing that she was able to turn the situation around by letting go of old grief.

If there's something going wrong in your life and you need a miracle, there's a great chance that karmic energy is standing between you and your miracle, so it's time to put in a call to the universe.

# Vibe of the day

Today, let the universe know that you are ready to release all the karma from your life now and your previous lifetimes in order to fulfil your current life's mission.

Know that if you have major regrets about your past, this karma will be taken from you, along with all the past-life karma you no longer need.

*'Divine universe, Lords of Karma,*

*Thank you for hearing my call!*

*I am willing and ready to release all the threads of energy that stand between me and my life's mission. Thank you for clearing all karma from my life today and any lifetimes gone by.*

*My soul is the purest aspect of me and I am ready for that purity and grace to flow through every aspect of my life.*

*I now clear, cancel and delete all old karmic bonds, energy and fear memories from my DNA, because it is my spiritual right to be free.*

*The karma is now abolished. I enter a new phase. So mote it be.'*

### #ShareYourVibe
*'Today I clear, cancel and delete the fears from my past!'*

# *Vibe 76* The violet cloak

There is a congregation of souls who have walked this Earth and are now working from heaven to help bring about change and healing in the world. They have been called ascended masters by many other authors, but I recently started to refer to them as 'the keepers of the light'. This title was inspired by a dream in which I visited an amazing kingdom and saw powerful love-focused beings of light sitting around a huge table.

One of these masters of wisdom is known as Saint Germain and he is the keeper of divine wisdom who helps us access our deeper sense of awareness. He is one of the lords of karma who help us disconnect from old karma and he looks after the spiritual energy known as 'the violet flame'. This is a powerful form of spiritual energy that we can draw on to overcome limitations. It can be invoked by anyone, of any religion, belief, creed or colour.

This keeper of the light was once known officially on Earth as Comte de Saint-Germain, which means Count of Saint-Germain, and was well received as a noble and a philosopher. There are some suggestions that he had royal blood and was possibly even a royal love-child, but there are many conflicting ideas as to his true bloodline. That being said, there is evidence that this man existed and was a real talent. He was one of those people who can turn their hand to almost anything – in his case, this included speaking several languages, playing musical instruments and having a deep knowledge of occult and spiritual matters.

As Saint Germain (which is his spiritual nickname) was multi-talented and spiritually connected, he can help you access the spiritual wisdom within you and express your talents. Not only that, he can help you be understood and accepted for who you are, no matter what your back story.

# Vibe of the day

It's time to draw down some masterly wisdom from a guide who is willing to help you. Today you can allow the support and wisdom of Saint Germain and the violet flame to come in and help you be the best person you can be.

It's important to know that today's lesson isn't only about getting all spiritually high-vibe and hanging out with cosmic masters in heaven – it's about recognizing that you deserve to receive wisdom, share your talents and be recognized and accepted for who you are without having to make any changes to yourself.

You can invoke the presence of Saint Germain at any time. Like the angels, he is a multi-dimensional being who can be everywhere at once.

You are offered the violet cloak of wisdom. Today it's time to put it on.

✦ Visualize yourself wearing a bright violet cloak. Imagine that it's like one of the huge capes that you see in Harry Potter movies. Let that awesome cloak cover your entire body.

✦ Then imagine that the violet energy of the cloak is filtering into your aura and shining out from it.

✦ Then say this:

*'Thank you, Saint Germain, for wrapping me up in your cloak of wisdom. I am ready to move beyond any limitations that may have been placed on me so that I can express*

*my gifts and talents. It feels so good to know my inner*
*wisdom is being highlighted with your guidance.*

*And so it is!'*

#ShareYourVibe
*'I deserve to be accepted for who I am.'*

# Vibe 77 Cosmic awareness

Hopefully by this point you are enjoying getting acquainted with the spiritual hierarchy of leaders, angels and teachers. They are all willing to help you because at a soul level you have chosen to be a light to this world.

Before you even came here you decided that you were going to be the positive force in the room, that you were going to heal your traumas (if you were faced with any) and that you were going to inspire others. It's almost as though before your soul came to your body you sat round a huge table with the keepers of the light and told them that you were willing to be that person and take on that mission.

Over the course of your life, you have had the choice to fall away from that decision. You may even have been led astray or faced your very own dark night of the soul. However, if you're reading this, you'll know that an SOS light within you began to flash and you answered to the call of your own spiritual self and decided that you were ready to change your thoughts, be a positive person and ultimately raise your vibration.

As you are raising your vibration, the keepers of light are backing you up with their support system and that support unit is dancing all around you. Right now a legion of angels is with you and they are angels of light. They respond to your prayers and direct you through your intuition – and they are so glad to be with you.

These angels can help you make the world a better place and today that's what you're going to do.

# Vibe of the day

Today's spiritual technique is all about service. You are a devoted helper of this world. You are a great giver and the angels want to honour you for it. Today is all about sharing the angels of light with people, places and situations you feel need a little bit of light.

Following a spiritual law known as grace, you are able to send these angels of light to people you love or even parts of the world you feel could be doing with healing miracles.

All you have to do in order for these angels of absolute light to help is imagine the purest whitest light surrounding the person (it can even be the most challenging person in your life), place or situation. You can then say something like this:

> *'Under the law of grace, thank you, angels of light, for surrounding [the person or situation] in your rays of peace, harmony and healing! May all soul(s) involved be touched by your divine hands.'*

#ShareYourVibe
*'Angels of light await your call!'*

# Vibe 78 Accessing the Earth star

The chakra system is an ancient spiritual system that has been passed through Sanskrit culture and the chakras themselves have helped us access the deeper aspects of our soul. As I mentioned earlier, although there are traditionally seven major chakras, in more recent times other chakras are being activated or acknowledged by humanity.

One of these chakras that is particularly important is known as the Earth star. I wrote about it in my book *Angel Prayers*. It acts as an anchor connecting us to the Earth. When I first pictured it on a clairvoyant level, I saw a huge crystal deep within the Earth and I could attach roots to it in order to feel more grounded and connected to our beautiful planet.

When it comes to spirituality, many people feel a need to access higher planes and different spiritual dimensions for guidance and inspiration – and I get why! But there are so many ways in which the Earth can support us and there's so much wisdom she can impart to us.

The Earth is a wise old soul. She's been here for millions of years. She's intelligent and she knows how to survive. She's been witness to so much and yet we never seem to think of approaching her for spiritual guidance or support.

When I teach people how to connect to the Earth, I spend time talking about her and sharing techniques like the lessons we shared in the 'Ground' sphere of the book to allow her support to enter their lives.

Taking time to connect to the Earth will enable you to be less clumsy, more in your body and more consciously aware of the part you have agreed to play while you are here. You chose to come to Earth, not to some other dimension!

# Vibe of the day

Take time today to get grounded. Accessing your Earth star chakra allows you to draw divine healing energy and support directly from Mother Earth. Allow her to impart her guidance and wisdom through a download of raw earthly energy with this simple meditation.

✦ Imagine that there are great roots going down from your feet to the centre of the Earth. See them travelling down through layers and layers of earth.

✦ When they reach the centre of the Earth, imagine them wrapping around a huge crystal of your choice and anchoring you right into the Earth.

✦ Take a deep breath and imagine copper light travelling up the roots into your feet and into your body. Know that this light represents earthly wisdom that you are dialling into.

✦ Spend some time feeling grounded and connected. You can even think about issues you need guidance on and imagine that your roots are like straws drawing love and support directly from the heart of Mother Earth.

✦ When you're ready, say:

*'I am connected to and aligned with Mother Earth.*

*Thank you, great mother, for aligning
me with my Earth star.*

*I am one with the Earth and I am grateful*
*for her support. We are one!'*

#ShareYourVibe
*'It feels so good to connect to Mother Earth!'*

# Vibe 79 Connecting to the soul star

There is twin energy to the Earth star and it's called the soul star. This chakra is the space where you can connect to the wisdom of your soul that has come down through lifetimes and lifetimes. It is seen clairvoyantly (or visualized) as a beautiful three-dimensional six-pointed star shining with magenta and rainbow light.

The soul star is a special chakra as far as I'm concerned, because it's the part of our spiritual anatomy that helps us remember on a soul level. This is what I've previously described as 'soul recognition' – when you see someone or something and it feels 'like home'. The reason it feels like home is because our soul is literally remembering a sacred part of us. It's the same thing when people have a spiritual experience or epiphany in a church.

I experienced soul recognition when I first discovered the angels. The feeling of warmth, excitement and connection was indescribable. When you get this feeling, the soul star is literally lighting up and coming into alignment with you.

Being open to connecting with the soul star will allow you to download insights and guidance and ancient spiritual memories from your soul so you can utilize the information here on Earth.

# Vibe of the day

Today you are encouraged to light up your soul star by thinking about where in your life you feel a sense of deep recognition.

Do you feel that you remember someone from lifetimes ago? Do you have a strong connection with a lover, friend or teacher that makes you feel like home? It could even be your child!

Is there a spiritual practice, technique or lineage that you connect with so deeply that it has to have been part of a previous lifetime?

Does thinking of a deity, great teacher or even the angels make your whole body come out in goosebumps?

Think now about what or who makes you feel at home. And as you do this, know that you are opening the channels to our soul star chakra.

Then set this intention:

*'I am willing to receive any memories or ancient knowledge from my soul that would be useful and supportive to the path I am on now.*

*Thank you, divine soul self-awakening now! I am ready to know you on a deeper level.'*

## #ShareYourVibe
*'When you meet someone and they feel like home, you are remembering something ancient.'*

# Vibe 80 Torch of light

There is another type of angel waiting to guide you to an even higher vibration: an angel of forgiveness.

Forgiveness is so important and it's going to keep coming up again and again in your life, but that's fine, because it creates so much space in your energy for miracles to enter.

Forgiveness is just about remembering the wholeness of your soul. It's the true awakening of your eternal self and the releasing of any stories in your life that aren't directing you towards love.

## Vibe of the day

Today's technique is simple. It's a self-enquiry.

Ask yourself:

✦ 'Who do I need to forgive?'

✦ 'Where in my life am I holding on to stuff that I don't need?'

✦ 'What's standing between me and feelings of freedom?'

✦ 'Is there anywhere in my life where I'm directing anger rather than focusing on what makes me feel loved?'

When you know the answers, you'll know what you need to do.

Say this:

*'Today I am ready to move to the next stage of forgiveness.
I allow this presence and awareness to direct me
forwards peacefully like a torch of blazing light.'*

And breathe. Cry. Do what you need to do. Let it all go!

# #ShareYourVibe
*'Forgiveness is an act of self-love because I let
go of anger that I don't need to feel.'*

# MANIFEST

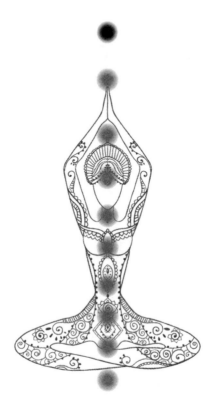

*Chakra:* The stellar gateway

*Location:* 30 centimetres (12 inches) above the head

*Colour:* Deep, deep space blue/purple

*Elements:* All

The stellar gateway is not only a spiritual energy centre but a vortex of light that allows us to access the creative matrix that is stored in the cosmos. We are then able to place our intentions into the heart of the universe in order for them to be created in our lives.

As we raise our vibration higher and higher, the stellar gateway responds to our perceptions, thoughts, actions and energy much more readily that it does when our vibration is low. This means that our levels of manifestation are much higher than normal, so it's important to have a sense of clarity about what we want to create.

In the lessons that follow, you are going to purify your energy and your perception in order to be in synch with your highest intentions. These will be less about particular goals or aspirations and more about bringing the life you love into reality.

 ## *Vibe 81* Creating space to allow

You have the ability to manifest miracles in your life. Remember, it's not about how big a miracle is but about how much room you've made for it. So when you set an intention, it's important to create space in that intention. Instead of wondering, 'When is this going to manifest?' or keeping looking at your email for that 'opportunity', just create space for it to happen.

Manifestation works seamlessly when trust is in place. But in order to have your dreams made manifest, you have to create space and then hand over whatever you're working on to the universe.

## Vibe of the day

You are encouraged to create space in your mind for the seeds of your dreams to grow. When you plant a seed in the garden, you don't dig it up to see if it's growing or not – you expect it to grow. So, trust in the universe. Know that whatever intentions you have put out into the field have been heard and that the wheels of this powerful universe are turning for your highest good.

Here's an affirmation:

*'My trust in the universe creates
space for my dreams to grow!'*

#ShareYourVibe
*'The universe loves it when we trust it!'*

# Vibe 82 Physical clutter = psychic clutter

When it comes to your life, everything in it represents your point of attraction. What that basically means is this: everything that you have, the way you look after your space, how you connect in relationships and how you present yourself to the world are how you present yourself to the universe.

Have you ever noticed that the person with the cluttered car is always running late? That the people with cluttered bedrooms are all over the place? Than an untidy desk or workspace creates a flaky, unorganized and unprepared colleague?

Physical clutter is psychic clutter and the universe is responding to it.

# Vibe of the day

It's time to make space in your life by tidying anything that needs tidying. Know that any mess or clutter in your physical world is influencing the energy you have now and the energy you are bringing into your life.

You deserve to experience seamless beauty in your life. What can you do to encourage this to happen?

Where in your life can you clear the physical clutter to clear the psychic clutter?

Get rid of the stuff you don't need (and sometimes that can be people). Clear out, clean up and get clarity.

Here's an affirmation to help you:

*'I keep a clean life to have clear energy!'*

> **#ShareYourVibe**
> *'Physical clutter is psychic clutter.*
> *I keep my space clear!'*

# Vibe 83 Embracing 'I am'

'I am' is a powerful statement (*see pages 15–16*). Every time you say 'I am' and then follow it with a word or sentence, you are literally drawing the energy connected to that word or sentence towards you.

So, what sort of energy do you want to draw towards you? How do you want to feel? How do you want to be perceived? How do you want to be supported?

Every single conversation you have internally and externally is influencing what is manifesting in your world. Everything you are experiencing on a personal level is an external projection of the experience you are having on an internal level.

When you say 'I am', know that you are drawing powerful universal energy into your life. Use this statement to enrich yourself and your world.

## Vibe of the day

Today you are encouraged to embrace your I AM-ness.

Create seven very personal affirmations that will boost your energy and rock your socks off:

'I am _____'

'I am _____'

'I am _____'

'I am _____'

'I am _____'

'I am _____'

'I am _____'

#ShareYourVibe
'I am a light to the world!'

# Vibe 84 Cosmic dancer

The universe is pulsing with energy right now. Surges of pure light potential are travelling far and wide through the cosmos. We are part of that cosmos and we get to decide if we will dance in harmony with that potential. Although the rhythm is subtle and probably on a level we can't fully comprehend, it's good to get on the dance floor with the universe.

We can dance with the universe in our actions, our thoughts and our behaviour. Instead of constantly trying to work out what's coming next or what's going to happen, we can just move to the beat of the universe.

There's an ancient image of the Hindu god Shiva known as Nataraja, which means 'Cosmic Dancer' or 'Lord of Dance'. Shiva is a powerful force – he's the god who destroys all fear. In his Nataraja form he's a man, generally with four arms, dancing in a circle covered in flames. This symbolizes Shiva destroying all the negativity in the world and making space for creation.

## Vibe of the day

Like Shiva, the Cosmic Dancer, you can awaken ancient energy within you in order to move beyond limitation and let go of all the negativity you don't need.

Put on music that you love and move in a way that feels powerful, strong, energetic and focused. Imagine that you are dancing with the universe. Know that the universe is swirling around you and dancing with you too.

As you focus your mind, begin to attune your energy to the pulses of the universe so it can help you to feel more aligned and able to trust in your journey from here.

#ShareYourVibe
'Today I dance with the universe,
knowing it supports my journey!'

## Vibe 85 Removing obstacles

Ganesh or Ganesha the elephant god is one of the world's best-loved figures of the divine. Originally a prominent figure in Hinduism, he is now loved by people all around the world.

Ganesh is revered as the remover of obstacles – he's the cosmic being that we can call on for help in moving beyond distractions and roadblocks to live the life we love and deserve.

I believe that although it's impossible for a human to have lived with an elephant head, it's definitely not impossible for a great sage or teacher in heaven to help us surmount challenges. For me, the idea of an elephant god isn't any stranger than the idea of an angel with wings – ultimately the image is just something for us here on Earth to focus on in order to form a connection with heavenly forces.

When I looked into the symbolism of Ganesh, I was amazed by the messages. His large ears represent the ability to be a great listener, his trunk symbolizes being able to adapt and be efficient, his big head helps us think big, he carries an axe to cut off all bonds or cords of fear, his one tusk represents retaining the good and leaving behind the bad, and there's so much more.

# Vibe of the day

Today you are encouraged to call on Ganesh to help you remove any obstacles that stand in your way – anything from stuck traffic to things taking ages, long queues or a sense that you aren't getting anywhere. Whatever the obstacle, the presence and energy of Ganesh can spur you on, as nothing can stand in his way.

Here's a prayer you can use:

*'Thank you, Ganesh, for removing all the obstacles that stand between me and my happiness. I now hand over to you anything that is a distraction from my sense of peace and contentment. Thank you for leading the way to my new beginning and raised sense of awareness.'*

You can also chant the traditional Ganesh chant:

*'OM Gan Ganapataye Namaha.'*

*(Sounds like: Ohhh-mmm Gahhn Gah-nah-pah-tah-yeh Nah-mah-ha!)*

This translates loosely to: 'Awaken, O sacred power of Ganesh, I welcome you!'

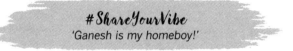

#ShareYourVibe
*'Ganesh is my homeboy!'*

# Vibe 86 The ruby ray

We've spoken about chakras all the way through this book because the chakra system is wonderful for helping focus our energy. The heart chakra, for example, is all about giving and receiving and is mostly seen as green. We can also draw down different colours from the universe to help us focus, refocus and expand our level of awareness. There are different spiritual rays that we can access to help us do this. In particular there is one that can help us reset, engage and activate our heart energy so we are aligned with a divine love energy that feels supportive: the ruby ray.

The ruby ray is a spiritual energy that represents divine love. It is looked after by an archangel known as Chamuel, whose name means 'He who sees God'. In truth, Chamuel helps us see the divine in everyone and everything.

Just like a ruby gemstone, the ruby ray is precious and three-dimensional in the sense that it sparkles in the light. The ruby is a stone of commitment, of undying love and passion. When you draw the ruby ray down into your heart centre, you make space within yourself to remember, reawaken and refocus the divine love with which you were born.

The ruby ray is perfect for working with at any time, but especially if you've had challenges in relationships, been let down countlessly by those you love and need to appreciate and love yourself more deeply.

# Vibe of the day

Draw the ruby ray down into your heart today. Set the intention to expand your experience of divine love and let Archangel Chamuel help you do it!

✦ Imagine that there is an amazing angel with you. Sense his tall, strong and protective physique standing behind you.

✦ This angel has a ruby in his hands and he places this ruby into your heart. Allow that energy to open up your heart space and remember the divine love that has never left you.

✦ Spend time meditating on this and when you're ready, say this affirmative prayer:

> *'Thank you, Archangel Chamuel, for connecting my heart centre to the ruby ray energy. I allow this light to enter me, awakening every aspect of divine love within my body, mind and soul. I am ready for an expansion on a heart level.*
>
> *And so it is!'*

### #ShareYourVibe
*'There is a divine love within me, which I choose to awaken!'*

# Vibe 87 The stellar gateway

You have now consistently lifted your vibration, focused your thoughts on love and overcome your own personal dramas. This 111-day thing may be a challenge and if you've had a few days off or have forgotten a few lessons, don't sweat. The fact that you've made it to this lesson shows that you're dedicated to your daily spiritual practice.

The stellar gateway is the next higher-energy chakra that you are about to align yourself with. It's found just above the soul star chakra and it's the centre that represents your ability to draw down support from the universe and literally manifest things in your life.

I like to imagine the stellar gateway as a mini Milky Way galaxy. It's the place that represents my connection to the universe, so I imagine it right above my head. It's a spectacular chakra that allows us to manifest our dreams, aspirations and goals by putting them into a vortex of universal energy.

## Vibe of the day

Connect to your stellar gateway and acquaint yourself with the energy of the cosmos today. Right now you have a mini-galaxy above your head that will act as a catalyst to your connection to the entire universe.

Rather than do anything with this energy it's just important to get your own energy high enough to feel it and feel comfortable with it. Although it's simple to connect to the stellar gateway, sometimes it can be overwhelming to feel its energy.

Set your intention:

> *'I am ready to connect to my stellar gateway.'*

✦ Take 10–15 minutes to meditate. Sit on the floor if you can to keep yourself grounded.

✦ With each and every in-breath, imagine that you are quite literally bringing the energy of the stars down into your aura.

✦ Keep this up and after around 20–30 breaths see yourself suspended (safely) in the heart of the universe – a space filled with pure potentiality. You are connected to the totality of possibilities.

✦ When you come back, move into a grounding posture like Child's Pose (*see page 49*), drink plenty of water and eat something grounding like rich dark chocolate to bring yourself back to Earth.

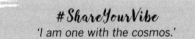

**#ShareYourVibe**
*'I am one with the cosmos.'*

# Vibe 88 **Manifesting miracles**

When you align with the stellar gateway, as we did in the previous lesson, you become even more attuned to your ability to manifest in real time, i.e. you set an intention and almost instantly you see it bear fruit. When this doesn't occur, you may think you've done something wrong. What could it be?

The only wrong thing you can do when manifesting is to fall into doubt and fear. But you can overcome this by turning on your miraculous mind.

The miraculous mind is the aspect of you that moves into the totality of possibility – that space of trusting that anything can happen, no matter its size or likelihood or how uncanny it would be if it did take place. The universe is a miraculous place, remember, and you deserve to work even more miracles into your life.

The miracle mind is amazing – it's one of trust and at times expectation, but it's also a mindset of sharing, service and dedication. It isn't about materialism, it's more about enjoying the nice things in life while remaining open to both success and what the world would call 'failure'.

With miraculous thinking, when something doesn't go 'to plan' you trust that your thinking, energy and ability to align with the universe are still bringing about the most amazing shifts in your life. The miraculous mind is the part of you that overcomes the doubt and fear mind – it's the part that relaxes knowing that there is an amazing shift occurring in the here and now.

## Vibe of the day

'I am one with the cosmos.
Living within the totality of possibility,
I trust that anything is possible.
Miracles occur naturally as I focus on plenty in my mind.
I am filled with universal potential, supported and guided.'

### #ShareYourVibe
'The mind is the medium for miracles!'

# ≡ *Vibe 89* **Purpose progression**

You've probably heard of past-life regression (and we're not doing it here), but there's a chance you may not have heard of future-life progression. Instead of going into a past life (which does work), I'm all about creating positive ideas and setting intentions *in the future*. After all, that's what's ahead of us, right?

In my own spiritual practice I do progressions where I move into a meditation and within that space allow myself to move forwards anywhere between five and 10 years. I remember when I first did a progression, when I was 15, I saw myself on a stage speaking to over 1,000 people about angels. I remember in the vision I came off the stage and Doreen Virtue, the world's most famous angel expert, came on right after me. I thought it was just my imagination. Well, it wasn't – in 2013 my vision came true.

Your mind has the ability to take you into the future too. What you will see will be based on your alignment and intentions now. Back then, my intention to do angel work was strong, and even though I lost my way with it for a few years, I got back on the horse with stronger intentions than ever, hence the manifestation coming together.

What are *your* thoughts and intentions focused on?

You can set intentions into your progression too! The universe reads these intentions as things that have already been created, and as long as they are for your highest good, it will deliver. So work it!

# Vibe of the day

✦ Move into your stellar gateway meditation as before (*see page 227*).

✦ Imagine you are suspended in the cosmos.

✦ Say something like 'I am ready to progress five years into the future' and allow your mind to show you some clips of maybe some of the things that will be happening five years from now.

✦ While you are there, you can put into place some of your goals for five years hence. Visualize them taking place and enjoy your progression, but do set the intention that you aren't attached to an exact plan and trust that the universe knows what is best for you. Take as long as you need to do this.

✦ When you're ready, imagine your intentions are a bright star. Place them in the cosmos and then send your stellar gateway into the heart of the universe.

✦ Your intentions are set. Now trust in the universe.

✦ Ground, breathe, eat and relax.

# #ShareYourVibe
'The universe makes the visions in your mind come true – focus well!'

# Vibe 90 Spread your wings

Something that I do to kick-start my vibes and help myself stay aligned with high energy is spread my wings.

You can create ethereal angel wings with your aura with a simple intention and arm movement. I took this from my experience in yoga and combined it with my angel work to create a positive flowing movement, which, alongside focused thought, will help you feel safe and empowered as you bring the life you love into manifestation.

## Vibe of the day

Today, open your ethereal angel wings!

✦ Bring your hands together at your heart centre in the prayer pose. Say: 'Thank you, angels, for opening my heart!'

✦ Keeping the prayer pose, move your hands to your throat area. Say: 'Thank you, angels, for helping me speak my truth with love!'

✦ Still in the prayer pose, bring your hands to your third eye. Say: 'Thank you, angels, for allowing me to have a clear inner vision!'

✦ Then raise your hands high above your head. Part them and draw wings in the air.

✦ Say: 'I spread my wings! I am free!'

### #ShareYourVibe
*'I spread my wings and do what I love!'*

# INTEGRATE

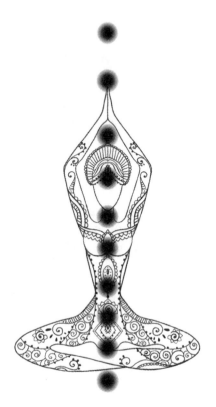

*Chakras:* All

The lessons become more focused and yet simpler in this section. They're all about encouraging you to delve deep into the simplicity of a daily spiritual practice.

You're encouraged at this point to integrate all of the lessons you've learned over the last 90 or so days and to take on board fully that you have the ability to raise your vibration just with some shifts in your thinking.

After each of the affirmations in this section, as short as they may seem, you're encouraged to sit for a while on your meditation pillow (or whatever you like to use) and allow the universe to deliver all the guidance and information you need.

Let the practice of sitting still and just allowing really unfold at this time so your ability to surrender to and trust in the universe can become a natural aspect of your life, spiritual practice and world.

Meditation tip: Let your palms face upwards so as to receive.

# Vibe 91 'I am supported on my path'

The vibrational lessons get easier here. You have raised your vibration. Now it's time to integrate what you already know.

## Vibe of the day

*'I am supported on my path.*
*Each step I take, I am guided.*
*I move with ease in life.'*

### #ShareYourVibe
*'Every step I take is guided!'*

# Vibe 92 'I am safe'

Knowing you are safe is important. You can never be hurt or broken – your soul is eternal. Today, claim your safety.

## Vibe of the day

*'I am safe.*
*My soul is eternal.*
*I am healed and whole.'*

### #ShareYourVibe
*'There's nothing that can stop*
*my soul from shining!'*

# Vibe 93 'I am a light'

When you remind yourself that you are a light, a huge beacon of energy begins to shine out from you. Angels, masters and all universal beings (including other lightworkers) are attracted to this light like magnets, so today attract your tribe of light!

## Vibe of the day

*'I am a light.*
*I am connected to the universal light source.*
*I am one with all other lights in the world!'*

# #ShareYourVibe
*'Today I choose to light up! Will you join me?'*

# *Vibe 94* 'I am strong and determined'

No one can get in your way but you. Today you are reminded to focus on your strengths, your gifts and the direction you are moving in. Let go of fear, drama and any other stuff that's getting in your way.

## Vibe of the day

*'I am strong and determined.*
*I move beyond all limitations.*
*I flow freely and effortlessly forwards.'*

# #ShareYourVibe
*'It's only fear that can hold you back. Let it go!'*

# *Vibe 95* 'I am kind to myself'

Speak to yourself the way you'd like to be spoken to. The negative words you've heard from others are probably things you've already said to yourself. All external negativity can be the echo of your own self-talk, so it's time to change that. Be kind and loving and gentle with yourself so the world can be too.

## Vibe of the day

*'I am kind to myself.*
*Today I find reasons to be kind to myself.*
*I offer myself the support I seek in others.*
*It feels good to be gentle.*
*Kind thoughts flow effortlessly through my mind.'*

#ShareYourVibe
*'I keep it kind in my mind!'*

## Vibe 96 'I am forgiven'

You don't need to ask for forgiveness from the divine – you are already forgiven. As soon as you make a mistake or regret something, the universe offers you love and compassion. But can you forgive yourself?

## Vibe of the day

*'I am forgiven.*
*I don't need to seek approval because I am already approved of.*
*The universe loves me already.*
*Thank you, universe. I accept that I am forgiven!'*

#ShareYourVibe
*'Forgiveness means less mess!'*

# Vibe 97 'I am accepted'

Knowing that you are a perfect child of humanity is important. Your angels, guides and all those you love in heaven love you very much. There is nothing you need to do or to be to make them prouder of you than they already are. They are over the moon that you are becoming the most positive you've ever been in your life. Today, move into the next wave of awakening through the feeling of acceptance.

## Vibe of the day

*'I am accepted.*
*The angels see me as divine.*
*I am accepted.*
*I choose to see my own light.*
*I am accepted.*
*Feeling at ease is my spiritual right!'*

#ShareYourVibe
*'I am nourished by being accepted!'*

# Vibe 98 'I am fulfilled by love'

According to all spiritual teachings, everything in this world is ultimately an illusion. Nothing material can return to heaven with you, so it's important to feel nourished and fulfilled by the one true energy that is mighty in both heaven and Earth: *love*.

Today, seek experiences that bring you closer to love and allow that energy to fulfil your every need.

## Vibe of the day

*'I am fulfilled by love.*
*It's the one true light in my life.*
*I am loved, loving and lovable.*
*Everywhere I go I experience love.'*

### #ShareYourVibe
*'Love is the answer.'*

# *Vibe 99* '**I am surrounded by angels**'

Angels draw close when you remember the presence of love. Like you, they are expressions of the divine and they are dedicated to your wellbeing. Know that your angels are present and you can experience their presence. Call on them and feel their loving guidance.

## Vibe of the day

*'I am surrounded by angels.*
*I am willing to feel their light.*
*I am grateful for their presence,*
*Their guidance day and night.*
*Protect me now, O angels of love,*
*Descend upon my life from up above!'*

### #ShareYourVibe
*'I am protected by angels!'*

# Vibe 100 'I am rooted to the Earth'

The more grounded you are, the greater the source of light you can be. Even though raising your vibration may give the impression that you're going to float into a new dimension, the truth is that you're lifting the energy of the one you're in. So stay rooted to Mother Earth – that way you can support others on this healing journey we're all on.

## Vibe of the day

*'I am rooted to the Earth.*
*My light is connected to the heart of the Earth.*
*I am grateful to be here!'*

### #ShareYourVibe
*'Staying grounded helps me become*
*a greater light to the world!'*

# ACTIVATE

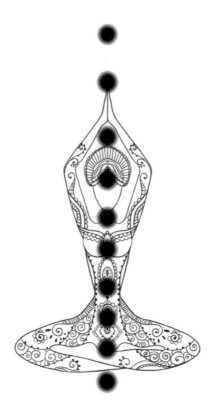

*Chakras:* All

It's now time for your light energy to be activated. This is all about creating new patterns and new habits in your life. Know that in this section you are raising all your chakras to the next level of awareness.

Your daily spiritual practice is about cultivating an awareness that helps you become the change you want to see in the world. If it is getting more focused, you should be able to see changes by now, especially when you are faced by challenges. Maybe where you would have overreacted and flipped out in the past you are now able to find a new way forwards.

Know one thing, though: this path takes a great deal of courage. Know another thing: angels of pure light are with you every step of the way.

All that you will do over the next 11 lessons will allow your integration with a higher vibration to be activated. This is your awakening! Prepare to shine brighter than ever before!

# *Vibe 101* 'I move with flow and ease'

A daily spiritual practice is about finding the balance between giving and receiving. It's about finding the middle ground between effort and effortlessness too, because too much effort can mean you get in your own way and effortlessness can make you miss what you're looking for. That middle ground is flow and ease.

## Vibe of the day

*'I move with flow and ease.*
*A wave of abundance washes over my life.*
*I am open to all levels of guidance and prosperity.*
*The universe supports every step I take.'*

### #ShareYourVibe
*'I go with the flow and I let my light show!'*

# Vibe 102 'I am ignited by life'

The universal life-force is an unlimited pool of energy. You are ignited by the presence of light. Today you are encouraged to breathe in the light and activate your will in order to feel connected to your divine plan.

## Vibe of the day

*'I am ignited by life.*
*I receive a constant flow of energy from the divine.*
*I allow my will to align with what is best.*
*I activate my light!'*

### #ShareYourVibe
*'It feels so good to be alive! My soul is ignited!'*

# Vibe 103 'I am open to receiving'

You are deserving of love. You don't have to look for it, just make space for it. Today you receive a kiss from the universe. Allow it to give it to you and to replenish all that you have given out.

# Vibe of the day

*'I am open to receiving.*
*My heart is open and receptive.*
*The universe is kissing my soul.*
*I welcome the infinite light of support.'*

## #ShareYourVibe
*'The universe gives when you choose to receive!'*

# Vibe 104 'I express my true self'

Your true self is your soul and ultimately it's a big bundle of love. Now I know you don't want to appear all fluffy and pink – you're so much more than that (for sure) – but it's time to really show your true colours. You are an amazing big bundle of stardust, of universal light and potential! It's time to own that and share it. Share yourself today and honour your vibes!

# Vibe of the day

*'I express my true self.*
*My true DNA is made of light.*
*My existence is miraculous.*
*I defy gravity every day.*
*I am an infinite being of love!'*

# *Vibe 105* 'I trust my inner vision'

Your natural self is clairvoyantly aware. Your mind constantly shares visions of support. Take time today to meditate, lock on to and connect to your inner vision. Your vibration blows through the roof when you follow its guidance – the guidance that always rests in the present moment.

## Vibe of the day

*'I trust my inner vision.*

*I allow the eye of my mind to awaken.*

*I am grateful for knowing when divine guidance is present.*

*I trust and follow my intuition with ease.*

*My soul is awake!'*

#ShareYourVibe
'Divine guidance arrives only in the present tense!'

# *Vibe 106* 'I honour the wisdom within'

There is a great chance you're inclined to follow your inner guidance at this time. You know you can trust it. You are always on the right path – you can never be off it. And you are encouraged to honour the wisdom within, while knowing you don't need to do anything dramatic. Guidance arrives softly and subtly, step by step.

## *Vibe of the day*

*'I honour the wisdom within.*
*Information and inspiration are given to me gradually.*
*I am guided every step of the way.*
*I am on the right path!'*

### *#ShareYourVibe*
*'You can never stray from the right path – every day is a lesson!'*

# *Vibe 107* 'I am part of the bigger picture'

The ego loves to convince you that you aren't good enough. It will have a plan for you to be a better person, but the truth is you're already doing your best. The universe wants you to know that you are part of the bigger picture. You are a catalyst for change and love – and everything you are doing is positively influencing the healing of the planet.

## Vibe of the day

*'I am part of the bigger picture.*
*My positivity is a catalyst for change.*
*I have every right to be here.*
*I accept healing for the world!'*

### #ShareYourVibe
*'Every step you take towards healing is helping the world.'*

## Vibe 108 'I am one with all that is'

The number 108 is an auspicious one in many different spiritual traditions, including yoga, Hinduism and Tibetan Buddhism. It is auspicious because it is the number of beads in both Hindu and Buddhist rosaries, known as *mala*. It's the number of Upanishads (spiritual texts) and *marma* points (a type of vital life point in Ayurvedic medicine). Not only that, the average distance from the moon to the Earth is around 108 times the moon's diameter and the average distance from the sun to the Earth is around 108 times the sun's diameter.

We can say that 108 is a number of oneness and of bringing together all that is. And yoga is the practice of uniting the body, mind and soul, so today let that be your practice.

## Vibe of the day

*'I am one with all that is.*
*I am made up of the life-force itself.*
*I can never walk this path alone because I am never alone.*
*I am connected to every person, plant and animal.*
*It is a blessing to be connected to the Source of creation.*
*It is a blessing to be an expression of light and life.'*

### #ShareYourVibe
*'We are all one. It's simple.'*

## Vibe 109 'I am embraced by light'

Lesson 75 of the *Course in Miracles* workbook says:

> **'The light has come. You can heal and be healed. The light has come. You are saved and you can save. You are at peace, and you bring peace with you wherever you go. Darkness and turmoil and death have disappeared. The light has come.'**

This explanation is a perfect representation of where you are today. You have worked the light into your system. You have upped your spiritual connection and raised your vibration and today you stand here as a beacon of pure light!

The light has come because you are that light. Today the universe bows in gratitude. Thank you for being that light. Today you are encouraged to be embraced by the light that you are.

### Vibe of the day

*'I am embraced by light.*
*I have removed all darkness.*
*The light has come.*
*I am a beacon of light!'*

#### #ShareYourVibe
*'Wherever I go, I choose to light up!'*

## Vibe 110 High vibes = high five!

Give me a high five. Don't just smile – I mean it. [Does a high five into the air.]

You have raised your vibes up high. I hope you know you have literally become an expression of your soul and the best light you can be at this time. Right now angels are gathering around you celebrating the fact that you have created radical shifts in your life.

You have aligned your chakras, connected to the universe, let go of any negativity and aligned with that which is most high. You are the bomb!

## Vibe of the day

*'My vibration is high.*
*I have moved up an octave.*
*I am connected with the Source that is most high.*
*Angels gather around me, lighting up the way.*
*Ascended masters and holy guides are with me now.*
*I am cruising along this path feeling led, high and connected.*
*It feels so good to feel so connected.*
*I was made for this!'*

### #ShareYourVibe
*'I don't walk my spiritual path, I rock!'*

# Vibe 111 'I am a lightworker – I have accepted my calling!'

Yep. You're officially a lightworker. You always were. You always will be.

Know that on some level you are being honoured. Imagine that a keeper of light is handing you a diploma and congratulating you, because that is what is happening.

You are here now and you have accepted your calling. Let's round up these 111 steps with this message for you from the divine:

# Vibe of the day

*'I am one with all that is.*

*Breathing, moving, expressing and receiving,*

*I inhale bliss, eternal prana, the energy of the cosmos.*

*As I exhale, I share this divine essence with the physical and non-physical dimensions around me.*

*My heart is part of one and all. It is the divine kiss on your forehead and the blood that flows through your organs.*

*Feel me in your centre, in your internal fire,*

*the cosmic inspirer awakening your will.*

*The divine power to change and create is alive, ready to manifest and share.*

*You are a star shining in the galaxy of my being.*

*It is your time to light up the world and the universe, because that is who you are:*

*you are the universe.'*

### #ShareYourVibe
*'I am a star shining at the heart of the universe!'*

# YOUR LIGHTWORKER DECLARATION

A declaration is a formal statement or announcement. When made in an affirmative style, it is able to lift your energy and empower your spiritual gifts and abilities.

You can make this declaration once or you can make it often (especially when you are having a down day or your ego is kicking you) to remind yourself that there is a higher purpose for you. You can say it out loud or silently. You can write it in your journal or on a bit of paper. Some people like to create their own ritual around this, while for others saying the words with feeling is enough. Choose what is right for you, because that is what spirituality is all about: creating your own unique relationship with the universe or whatever name you give to the source of your creation. I sometimes keep it simple by just calling it *love*.

In the blank spaces, say your name or, if you own this copy of the book, please write it directly into it.

When you have finished your declaration, take some time to breathe and receive.

# Declaration of a lightworker

I, _____, am ready to accept that there is a greater purpose for my life. I am willing to accept that within me there is a divine spark of light that will never cease to be.

I recognize and accept that the path of a lightworker is not a solo path but one that is lit up by the presence of the divine itself and the angels of light.

I am _____

I am a lightworker.

I choose to accept that I am a soul. My soul is resilient, strong and guided. The voice of my soul is loud, clear and supportive.

I am supported by 100,000 angels and archangels.

The ascended masters who have walked this path before me are cheering me on because they have recognized that I am ready to inspire change and acceptance.

I am _____

I am a light.

The world is lighting up now.

I choose to contribute to that light.

I choose to see and recognize that light.

As the light of the lightworkers joins together as one, may all those in need be touched by the peace that we feel in our hearts. May they experience joy and acceptance in their world.

We are the light.

In grace I accept the mission of a lightworker and I declare that I have heard my calling.

Thank you, angels, for lighting my way.

Thank you, teachers and lightworkers who have ascended. I welcome your guidance and support.

Thank you, great source of creation. I am glad we are doing this together.

And so it is.

# ABOUT THE AUTHOR

Drew John Barnes

**Kyle Gray** has had spiritual encounters from an early age. When he was just four years old, his grandmother's soul visited him from the other side.

Growing up, Kyle always had an ability to hear, feel and see what goes beyond the natural senses, which eventually led to him discovering the power and love of angels in his teens.

Now, at just 28, Kyle is one of the most hip and sought-after experts in his field. With his unique ability to stay grounded and keep it real, he reintroduces the idea of angels and spirituality in an accessible way and believes he can bring ancient spiritual knowledge across in a modern way to help the reader of today.

Kyle speaks all around the world, and his talks in the UK and Europe have been known to sell out. He is based in Glasgow, Scotland, where he runs his boutique Yoga & Meditation studio, The Zen Den.

**f** **kylegrayuk**

**🐦** **@mgck**

**📷** **@mgck**

**www.kylegray.co.uk**

# HAY HOUSE

*Look within*

Join the conversation about latest products,
events, exclusive offers and more.

**f**    Hay House UK

🐦    @HayHouseUK

📷    @hayhouseuk

♥    healyourlife.com

*We'd love to hear from you!*